Petit's Tours of Old Staffordshire

Petit's Tours of Old Staffordshire

Philip Modiano

RPS Publications

Published by RPS Publications
www.revpetit.com
enqiries@revpetit.com

Distributed by YPS
orders@yps-publishing.co.uk

Copyright © 2019 Philip Modiano

ISBN 978–1–9164931–0–0

Designed by Sally Salvesen
Printed by AB Spauda, Vilnius, Lithuania

A catalogue record for this book is available from the British Library
10 9 8 7 6 5 4 3 2 1

All the watercolours illustrated are by the Reverend J. L. Petit and in private collections, unless otherwise stated.

Frontispiece: Croxden Abbey, c. 1839

Contents

Preface

I first came across the Reverend John Louis Petit only a few years ago and was surprised to find that a man who seemed to be such a good artist was practically unheard of, or, worse, was damned with faint praise. Gradually, as I dug further, it became clear that the dismissers had little clue about the real Petit: not only a uniquely expressive artist but also so much more than an artist; he had been an important, even heroic, opponent of the Gothic Revival; and he was the first significant advocate for the preservation of ancient buildings, decades before others such as William Morris. Surely he deserved better, but how best to redress the balance?

Rather than write a traditional book about a Victorian artist, I chose this tour/treasure hunt format in the hope that it will appeal not only to those who already appreciate heritage but also to those who want an inviting way to start. Architecture – especially our oldest church buildings – is what drove the Reverend Petit to paint. It affects us all, and we can see it best if we look at it on the spot.

Petit was an important man 150 years ago both as artist and architectural critic, but after his death his reputation was destroyed by his opponents, and until recently nearly all his art lay hidden, forgotten and deteriorating. Practically nothing useful had been written about him. Academic articles have their place and are being written, but Petit's story seemed to appeal to everyone to whom I have told it. And for reasons that will become clear, the best way to introduce Petit is in his home county of Staffordshire, one of the finest counties of Victorian England.

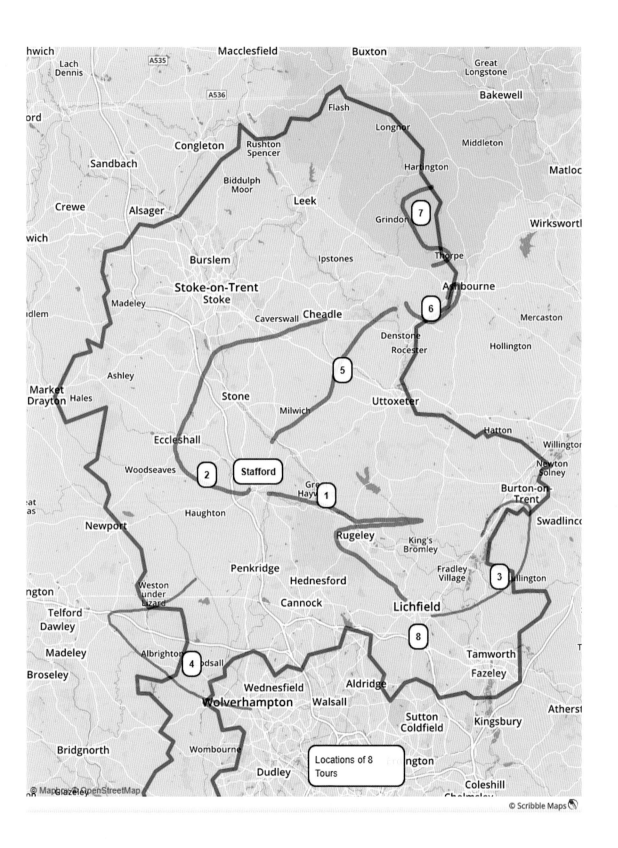

Locations of 8 Tours

o.1. The Reverend J. L. Petit, c. 1865, 34 × 24. This photograph is likely to have been taken by Petit's friend, Philip Delamotte. Image courtesy of William Salt Library, Stafford.

Introduction

This is a book about the Victorian artist the Reverend John Louis Petit (1801–68), about Staffordshire, and about architectural character. It is both an art book and a guidebook.

Staffordshire used to be the centre of the Kingdom of Mercia, the greatest of the English kingdoms for 300 years from 600 to 900 AD. Lichfield was an archbishopric. Even as recently as Victorian times Staffordshire was famed for its natural beauty, especially the hills and vales in the north of the county; and envied for its natural resources, especially coal, iron and clay. But its status has been declining now for over 100 years. Reduced in size and wealth by the loss of the Black Country, non-residents mostly transit through it on the trunk roads that bisect it.

The Reverend Petit, one of Staffordshire's greatest artists, was more than just an artist. He was the leading opponent of the craze for Neo-Gothic in architecture that swept all before it, including precious medieval churches. He advocated preservation wherever possible twenty years before that became accepted. He also advocated originality in architecture as opposed to imitation, and sought with his art to demonstrate the beauty in all old styles in Britain and abroad. For twenty years from around 1840 to 1860 Petit was at the centre of the most remarkable architectural debate that has taken place in Britain – 'the battle of styles' which gradually softened the destructive force of the most extreme Gothic supporters, although not to the extent that Petit would have wished.

As an artist Petit was never commercial, painting to sell; he painted scenes and buildings accurately, without taking artistic licence to 'improve' the scene as professionals were wont to do. He painted to communicate the character, and the effect on the observer, of the building as it was, and occasionally landscapes, or just for his own pleasure, all of which only contributes to the exceptional nature of his work. But after his death practically all his art remained hidden until recent times.

So it seems appropriate that Staffordshire and Petit combine together, allowing us to visit some beautiful and interesting places before they are lost, and revisit some old but fundamental arguments about beauty and preservation in our heritage, and what makes for good building, which are as relevant today as then.

The rest of this introduction sets the scene in a more detail.

STAFFORDSHIRE IN 1834 – AT A PEAK IN ITS FORTUNES

By a stroke of good luck William White wrote his *History, Gazetteer and Directory of Staffordshire* in 1834 which is within a few years of when Petit's earliest paintings can be dated. The *Gazetteer* lists just about anything of importance parish-by-parish, hundred-by-hundred (Staffordshire contained five hundreds in those days, important sub-divisions above the parish and below the county level). It is a kind of Domesday book for that moment in time, and we can see what a well-endowed county it was.

Following the development of the canal network in the eighteenth century, Staffordshire was ideally placed between the industrial areas of the north and the commercial capital. It had the third-biggest manufacturing sector after Lancashire and Yorkshire, centred on Wolverhampton and Stoke, while the rest of the land was fertile, pastoral or picturesque.

The 1830s, and the mid-Victorian period that was to follow, were as full of change as our times. The introduction of the railways would cut journey times hugely – the first of several transport improvements that gradually led to the current situation where Staffordshire can be by-passed. Increasing trade and international commerce would eventually undermine its industrial base of metal work to the south and potteries to the north. The biggest change, of course, was the carving out of its main industrial region around Wolverhampton, which was a vital part of Staffordshire in the nineteenth century.

A by-product of these changes was the disappearance of many wealthy families, and the decay of many of the 'seats of nobility and gentry' for which the county was also famed, and this we will see as we compare the pictures of those days with today. Family lines fail everywhere but the fact that Staffordshire would seem to have suffered a large net loss, from moves out of the county and fewer replacements, is likely to have been a consequence of its relative economic decline.

However, Staffordshire's churches, cathedrals and monuments can hold their own even against those of Yorkshire or Gloucestershire; its towns and cities – Lichfield, Stafford and Burton-on-Trent – are still as attractive as many better-known county towns. The rivers Trent, Dove and the others; Cannock Chase and the Peaks and Moors all make Staffordshire one of the best-kept English secrets lying in plain view, even if it is not now famed for tourism.

THE GOTHIC REVIVAL – WHY IT MATTERED

The roots of the Gothic revival can be traced back well into the previous century. Horace Walpole, son of the first Prime Minister, transformed his house in Twickenham, Strawberry Hill, into a mock gothic castle, in the 1750s. The attraction to Gothic architecture would grow hand in hand with the Romantic movement for the next 100 years, but until 1820 or so the number of buildings using the style, even churches, was actually rather small. This was to change.

In Victorian times, in addition to the need for railway stations and town halls, with the exploding population and wealth many more churches were required too. Also there were the resources and motivation to repair the older ones. The Government allocated funds for 214 in 1818, and of these 174 ended up being Gothic in style. But many more were built privately, with over 3,700 consecrations from 1820 to 1875, nearly all Gothic. For the Government churches Gothic was apparently a cheaper option, but the predominance of Gothic for privately funded churches demonstrates a remarkable conformity. Already well established by 1839, after that it became not enough to build Gothic but exactly what kind of Gothic became matters of intense, aggressive debate.

Historically, churches were then and still are by far our most important architectural heritage. In Petit's words: 'In every country the temples devoted to worship are the richest, the most durable, and the most beautiful, among the structures remaining to us.'

They were and are the embodiment of communities, and the centres of power and tradition. Most of them were originally Catholic, then became Protestant after the Reformation; but many

0.2. The Weaver Hills from Ellastone, 1838, 21 × 27. This view is included in tour 6.

0.3. St Mary's, Stafford, 1843, 23 × 29. Courtesy of Staffordshire Museum Service. Petit opposed unnecessary changes to the structure of medieval churches, and often drew them to capture their character before alteration. More details and pictures of this church are in tour 2.

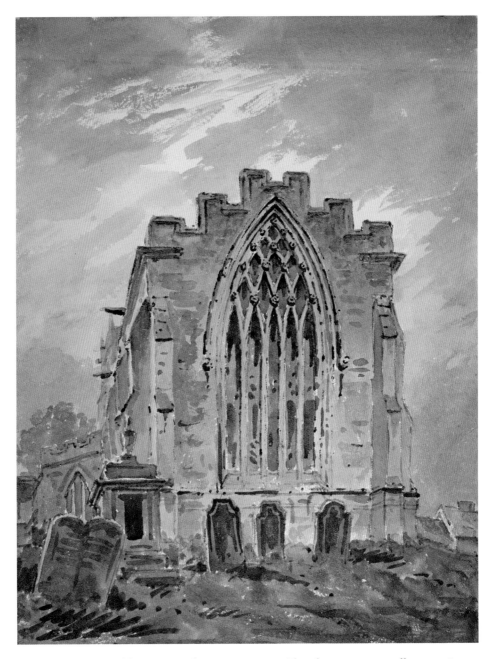

0.4. St Mary's, Checkley, east window, 1838, 36 × 26. This shows an unusually attractive window, which Petit found in a local parish church in mid-Staffordshire, part of tour 5.

are built on sites of worship even older than Christianity. Many were sorely in need of repair and restoration, but the manner of doing so was hotly contested. The advocates of Gothic, after 1839 mostly followers of Pugin, believed in one 'correct style' which they defined very narrowly, but not consistently. The Ecclesiologists (or Cambridge Camden Society to give them their proper name) would go to great lengths to criticize architects who did not follow their recommendations, and those who wanted work were influenced by them. For a time in the 1840s they argued for 'destructive' renovation, i.e. the rebuilding of churches and even cathedrals to conform to this one correct style. Against them stood a mixed grouping of gentleman antiquarians and other intellectuals, who were appalled at the loss of ancient, albeit untidy, buildings and resisted on principle the imposition of 'one correct style' by a self-appointed clique.

It should not be too difficult for us to imagine the intellectual battle that took place, in public, in journals, public speeches and books, during the 1840s and 1850s, and which forms the backdrop of Petit's career as an artist and architectural critic. It is true that without social media participation was restricted, however the formation of 100 or so architectural and archaeological societies up and down the country illustrates its importance.

Architecture was just emerging as a profession – something all educated men (and some women) engaged with – rather than being left to professionals as is the case now. In the early part of the nineteenth century there were still only two universities in England (i.e. excluding those in Scotland and Ireland). The third and fourth, Durham and University College London, were just starting up. All Oxford and Cambridge undergraduates studied theology, and nearly one half went on to take holy orders. Apart from the military and government service, it was what educated folk often did. Competition for livings (i.e. a vicarage, where the incumbent was entitled to keep the money raised in the parish) was fierce. Once obtained a vicar could hold his position for life, if need be, and the work could be sub-contracted to a curate for a fraction of the living.

Many Victorian gentlemen, clergymen or not, devoted time to intellectual pursuits. Striving to do something useful was entirely genuine, and the effort put in is astonishing. Hours, days and weeks were carefully sub-divided and organised, leaving only a little space for correspondence with colleagues across the country, religious observance on Sundays, and formal dinners. The question of how to restore the old, and in what style to build new buildings of all kinds, and churches in particular, was absolutely central to this intellectual class; as it was their responsibility to manage the heritage bequeathed to them and that they would bequeathe to future generations. This was the battle Petit took up.

Enter the Reverend John Louis Petit

Petit was born in 1801 to a comfortably wealthy family of Hugenot descent; he followed in his father's footsteps, taking holy orders in 1826 and working until 1834 as a curate, before quitting to concentrate on his twin vocations of painting and architectural writing and criticism.

Because he was not a commercial artist few now know of him. His art was displayed, up to one hundred works at a time, mainly to support his speeches about architecture. It acted as a huge draw, but then disappeared after his death. Stored and ignored by descendants for 130 years it was accidentally abandoned to new owners. These, ignorant of their find, dumped the hoard into regional auctions in huge quantities, unsorted, carelessly mixed up with lots of weaker pictures by Petit's sisters. Many have been lost. Little wonder that only now, with research, we are slowly realizing what an extraordinary artist he was.

Petit's early pictures, until 1841 when his architectural career took off, include numerous landscapes, of which many are in Staffordshire. In later years he travelled and painted, increasingly

0.5. Noyon, France, 1855, 24 × 34. Some of Petit's most beautiful pictures show the effect of a church in its landscape, with many examples from France and the UK dating from the mid-1850s.

obsessively, to record examples of church architecture across Europe. He especially liked to capture the church-in-its-landscape, showing how it fitted its setting (see example: Noyon).

He mostly did close-up architectural sketches, which he used for his writing and speaking – often interesting (see example below: Corfu), but latterly only a few were subsequently finished with colour. His sisters, especially Emma, often painted alongside him. Frequently he would visit a church to capture its character in the knowledge that a restoration project was about to start.

Many sketches have found their way onto the market, but few completed watercolours. Almost none of the pictures in this book have been seen in public before. Indeed it is a small miracle that these made it, when so many, as well as his papers, appear to have been lost and destroyed through damage in poor storage conditions.

The proportion that have come down to us forms an extraordinary topographical collection. In volume his output was not unique, because other gentlemen left thousands of topographical

0.6b. Corfu church. Illustration in an article by Petit, on Byzantine architecture in *Archaeological Journal* 1866, exactly copying his watercolour from nine years earlier.

0.6. 'All Saints, Corfu', 1857, 38 × 27. This is in fact SS. Jason and Sossipatro, the oldest Byzantine building in Corfu. Architectural sketches, close-ups of churches or details of churches were drawn mainly to support his speaking and writing.

drawings. But in quality as well as quantity he is. Free from the artifices of professional artists who adjusted what they saw to create a 'picturesque', saleable scene, Petit captures the effect, truthfully, as it was – the power and majesty of Lichfield Cathedral, on the cover; the tragedy of the old monasteries (see Iona, below); or the dignity and rootedness of the humble parish church.

Yet, from the 1840s on Petit viewed his primary career as being an architectural writer and commentator, and his art from this time on, outside Staffordshire and abroad, mostly provided the illustrations for what he wanted to say. In his writing and speaking against the Gothicists, Petit was one of the first to try to articulate, and show, what made buildings beautiful, characterful (I explain more of how Petit developed the idea of a building's character in the book) and appropriate; how age contributes to dignity, how different forms and proportions can look and feel right. The preservation of a church's character, and the impossibility of imitating the true character of medieval gothic, was what Petit argued with his art. While 'beauty', 'dignity', 'character' may all seem intangible, in

0.7. Iona, Inner Hebrides, Scotland, 1857, 27 × 37. Petit drew this several times on his visit, both close up and from wider angles, capturing the effect of the scene as well as being topographically accurate.

fact he and the other antiquarians considered they were the side of reason and science, opposing the irrational dogma that was imposing arbitrary rules for others to follow and decreeing what was correct or not. Petit's approach of gathering numerous images to illustrate his points is a typical example of the Victorian empirical approach to otherwise hard-to-pin-down concepts.

Landscape and nature, which he loved, became a far less frequent subject after 1840 during these years of conflict. Yet, for Petit, nature, God's works, in its infinite variety of harmonies was the model to inspire architecture. And, as with his architectural paintings, he strived to be accurate and capture drama and effect in his landscapes.

If Petit devoted his life to understanding, explaining and preserving architectural beauty, its forms and proportions, and its diversity, his focus on churches should not put anyone off. His works can be valued and admired by people of any faith and none as the heart of the land in which you see them.

A more detailed biographical chapter is included after the tours.

0.8. Winter scene, near Stowe, Lichfield, 1855, 27 × 37. The exact location is not known. It forms part of a group of snow scenes painted in February 1855, three of which are included in tour 3.

The Tours

Here, then, are eight tours of interesting and beautiful places in old Staffordshire depicted by Petit in watercolour one hundred and fifty years ago. Treasure hunts of a kind. I show you the pictures, and guide you to the spots where he sat to compare the past with the present. Each tour visits around seven places, in about an hour's journey time, and so can be completed easily in a few hours including stops to find the angles and compare the view with the picture.

Geographical groupings have taken precedence over biographical order, so as to make nice-sized tours. There are also a few challenges, such as the winter scene shown here or the distant view of St Peter Wolverhampton below, where I have not found the exact spot; and each tour contains at least one 'mystery picture'.

Architecture is often called the hardest art form of all, and one where non-professionals' opinions are frequently discounted. Comparing a building as it was one hundred and fifty years ago with what is visible now will help everyone to understand the concept of architectural character and be

0.9. Near Wolverhampton, c. 1835, 11 × 25. The area is now still parkland, West Park, but the views are blocked by buildings and trees.

more confident in their opinions. While Petit was both artist and architectural critic, and I include brief descriptions of points he was making, the balance in this book is firmly towards his art, using that as a way to start to appreciate the architecture he wanted to illustrate.

I have taken a few liberties with the border in order to bring in interesting and connected places which happen to fall just across it. The southernmost tour (4) starts in Wolverhampton, a part of Staffordshire in Petit's day, and nibbles into Shropshire to take in the important Petit subjects of Shifnal and Tong. Three of the other tours include a few pictures just over the border with Derbyshire, because they are close and related.

In tours 6 and 7 in the north east of the county, you could make use of walking boots. Tour 7 in particular involves a couple of longish walks to reach sites. But even in those most points can be viewed from within fifty metres of a parked car.

None of the tours has to be followed in the order given, and you can pick and choose from among them if you prefer to construct your own itinerary. The maps should be enough for that. The first tour includes more information than the others, so it is the best place to start.

Yet, this is an art book, and an architecture and conservation book, not just a tour guide, and so it can also be read without setting foot outside.

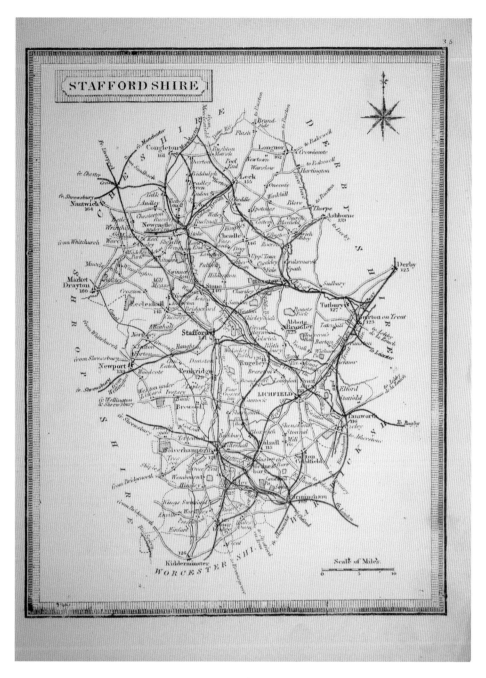

0.10. Mid-nineteenth-century map of Staffordshire, 19 × 15, showing the canals and railways.

1.1a. Tixall Gatehouse, c. 1835, 29 × 25. This watercolour was used as the basis for the opening illustration in Petit's first publication, *Remarks on Church Architecture* (1841). It is one of very few which are not ecclesiastical architecture.

Tour 1

Between Stafford and Lichfield: Overview and Architectural Character

All of the tours are varied, but tour 1 covers all Petit's artistic styles, all types of subjects (though only one church) and is probably the most easily accessible geographically for many readers. So it serves as an introduction to the other tours, and I add more context.

We start just outside Stafford, 6 miles and 15 minutes from junction 13 on the M6, for a specific reason. The picture on the facing page was the subject of the first illustration in Petit's first book – *Remarks on Church Architecture* (called *Remarks*) published in 1841. It seems no coincidence that he chose Tixall Gatehouse to mark his entry into his chosen field, and so I can do no better than start here too. *Remarks* is a tour de force in two volumes with over 300 illustrations of some of the most beautiful churches from across Europe, all of which he had visited and painted himself, as well as

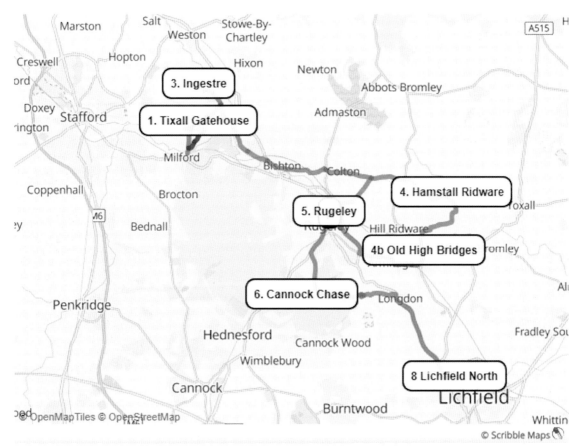

then doing line drawings copying each watercolour in preparation for the illustrations in the book.

As explained in the Introduction, by the late 1830s Gothic had long been favoured for new churches, and the fashion was about to become even less tolerant of alternatives. For a period restoration was even to replace non-conforming styles. Petit set out to oppose this.

'I have done my best to set before the reader a sufficient variety, both in form and composition, to prove to him how wide a range can be taken by architects….to be confined neither to one country, nor one age, nor one scale of importance', in other words for all churches lets not just copy English fourteenth-century gothic.

Actually Petit liked the *old* Gothic, he just felt that it should not be copied but architects should use all styles to create something original: 'little beauty will result from the imitation of details.' He was particularly appalled by destructive restoration: 'it is truly grievous to see the proportions of a beautiful edifice needlessly defaced…or the character swept away by persons who follow only such rules as are dictated by their own caprice or fancy…'

Obvious now, this was heresy at the time and he was lambasted, and praised, in equal measure. The criticism became quite personal but he stuck to his arguments with unfailing politeness, and not a little heroically. The arguments around these ideas, and Gothic in particular, continued for the rest of his life.

1.1. TIXALL GATEHOUSE, ST18 0XT

Just past Tixall village along the Tixall road outside Stafford, lies what is among the most remarkable gatehouses in the country. Perhaps one of the least visited buildings of national importance and the subject of one of the most evocative of Petit's pictures. Coming from Stafford it is easy to drive past without seeing it because of the way the road bends and with the woods just before it.

At present one can park in front of a gate to the field in which it stands (if no one else is there), but the exact spot where the picture was drawn is along the boundary beside the woods.

The picture (p. 20) probably dates from about 1835. The dramatic angle is typical Petit from this date on. It captures exactly the feelings evoked by the building, a brilliant architectural monument standing alone and completely out of place in its field. Currently it is owned by the Landmark Trust and can be rented by the week. It is not clear to me why it was not more frequently painted and why it is not a recognized tourist destination, but we can enjoy it all the more for that.

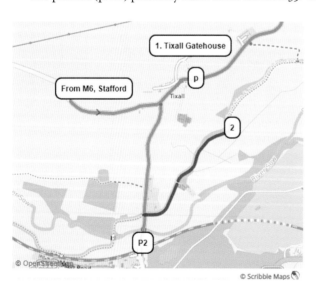

Petit included the gatehouse in *Remarks* as an extraordinary example of 'cinquecento', sixteenth-century architecture, characterized by its layers and elaborate decorative façade, far different from traditional gothic, but its symbolism as an

1.1b. Tixall Gatehouse, illustration published 1841. This image appears on p. 14 of vol. 1 of *Remarks*, showing how closely Petit's original watercolours were copied when used as illustrations.

TIXALL GATEWAY.

entry point seems more important. Tixall Gatehouse is even more extraordinary today as it stands a lonely guard of the vision that created it four hundred years ago – the main house having long since been demolished. Unlike some of our destinations, this is one where the current view holds up very well in comparison with the picture.

We will see more pictures from Petit's first book especially in tour 5, although none as dramatic as this.

1.2. NEAR TIXALL – HOLDIFORD LANE
(20 minute dead-flat walk)

This picture was made along the Stafford canal which parallels the River Sow, tributary of the Trent, at a place called Tixall Wide. The tops of the gatehouse are just visible, centre left in the picture. Even the vegetation has not changed much and the scene is practically the same as it was 180 years ago.

Approach it by returning into the village of Tixall, taking the left turn down Holdiford Lane towards Milford and cross first the canal bridge and then find parking just after the river bridge on the left. The entrance to the canal is beside the canal bridge on the other side of the road. There is a nice plaque detailing local attractions, but why

1.2. Near Tixall, 1830s, 16 × 21. An earlier, more-conventional landscape from the canal. The domes of the Gatehouse are visible to the left of the trees in the picture.

could they not manage to create a small place to park easily? The walk along the canal bank is pleasant, but longer than ideal because there is no public access at Tixall Lock, the first place one reaches after 5 minutes' walk. Continue to the second left-hand bend after the lock to start to see the gatehouse in the distance on the left. Probably best done before mid-Spring, as I did, when vegetation is less. It is a beautiful location, similar to the picture, with gorgeous egrets (slender herons) in full plumage to add to the scene. One can see more or less exactly where the artist must have sat.

The picture dates from the 1830s and is from a different, earlier, album than that of the gatehouse in which dark monochrome prevailed. Already his style is more natural than typical Victorian landscapes, which can seem quaint and formal, from all but the best artists. We will see many other landscapes from the 1830s in all the more northerly tours.

The canal was a key route linking the Trent and Severn rivers and vital for trading goods from Wolverhampton and from the Potteries. By 1830 it was operating 24 hours a day. It stayed privately owned until 1947, and was saved from closure in 1959 by the Staffordshire and Worcestershire Canal Society. It has been a Conservation area since 1969. The whole scene is probably much more attractive now than it was when in full use. Chalk one up for the present.

1.3 Ingestre Hall, st18 0rf

Return back past the gatehouse, Ingestre is only three miles away. This picture is in the Staffordshire County Museum collection, and dates from the late 1820s or early 1830s.

In the 1820s Ingestre Hall was owned by the Chetwynd family, Henry Chetwynd-Talbot, Viscount Ingestre, later third Earl Talbot. Petit's third sister, Mary, married Henry Chetwynd, third son of Sir George Chetwynd, a relative who lived a few miles away in Brockton Hall on the other side of Tixall. Since Henry and Mary's marriage took place in 1827, it is possible that the picture dates from this time. Earl Talbot went from strength to strength during the Victorian period. In 1860 the Earl of Shrewsbury, a distant cousin 15 generations back, died in Alton, site of Alton Towers (see 5.7); Henry, Earl Talbot, fought off a couple of rivals (legal battles not fisticuffs), to win that inheritance and became the eighteenth Earl of Shrewsbury, as well as acquiring a number of other subsidiary titles (e.g. Earl of Waterford) to add to those he already had. Meanwhile Henry Chetwynd, Petit's brother-in-law, was not doing so well; he and Mary borrowed money from Petit, which Petit forgave in his will.

The eldest son of the Earl is still called Viscount Ingestre, but the family disposed of the estate in 1961 with the condition that it be used to promote the arts. The Hall is now a residential arts centre owned and managed by Sandwell Metropolitan Borough Council, so as a school, visitors are not allowed on the grounds. However, the nearby Orangery is developing into a public access heritage site, and you can drive alongside the old Christopher Wren church, to access that and see the façade to the left from the road. The house was built in 1613, a little later than the gatehouse that we have just visited, and similar in style.

Family was of primary importance, without Government services to rely on. Petit was the eldest of ten children, with two brothers and seven sisters. Only he and four sisters married, three

1.3. Ingestre Hall, 1830s, approx 23 × 33. Courtesy of Staffordshire County Museum Service.

of whom had children. Ultimately nearly all of Petit's work went to a nephew, son of his youngest sister, Maria.

Other family-related pictures are below (1.7) and in tours 3 and 8. We will visit three more estates, two in tour 5, one of which is indeed Alton.

1.4. Hamstall Ridware, St Michael and All Angels, WS15 3RT

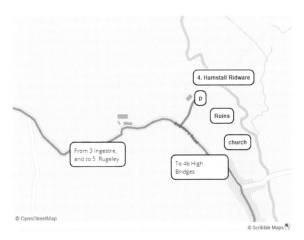

Next we go to Hamstall Ridware, an easy drive to one of the quirkiest villages in Staffordshire, about 11 miles and 20 minutes distance. It is the scene of a minor tragedy which becomes clear when you compare the present scene with the picture. The picture below – at least 70% of it – can be seen if you turn off Blithbury Road (above postcode) down the poorly made-up road signed to Tollgate House Farm, north of the Hall. While the buildings to the right in the picture, including the old Hall, have been redeveloped into several beautiful houses, the

1.4a. Hamstall Ridware, c. 1836, 19 × 28. Painted from Toll Gate Farm Road, this is the most successful of the group; it shows the entire cluster of buildings as it was.

1.4b. Hamstall Ridware Gate, c. 1830s, approx 22 × 28. Courtesy of Staffordshire County Museum Service.

gates and old tower have been left to crumble away.

There are four villages with Ridware in their name close to each other: Hamstall, Pipe, Hill and Mavesyn. The name has Celtic (Rid-) and Saxon origins, and predates the Norman Conquest. Subsequently the local Saxon thane adopted the Norman-ish name 'de Ridware', and quite remarkably, his family managed to keep the manor intact for a few hundred years more until 1370.

While the Church dates from

1.4c. Hamstall Ridware Tower and Church, c. 1830s, 19 × 13. Probably the earliest of the group, judging by the slightly lesser extent of ivy on the tower.

1.4d. Hamstall Ridware Tower and Church, c. 1830s, 27 × 19. The old watch tower was in much better health and over-dominates this and the smaller version above.

early Norman times, Hamstall Hall, and the remarkable gate date from the early seventeenth century. I have not found a date for the old watchtower, which adds so much to the character of the group. In Petit's day the village had 440 inhabitants, about the same as now, and the Hall was rented out to a local farmer.

Petit painted here at least three times in the 1820s and 30s, but does not appear to have done so in later years when he focused on church architecture. On the earliest trip he struggles to find a good composition which captures both tower and church spire (see 3rd and 4th pictures). The second picture, just above, captures the gate, and is more successful. But it is the first picture of the group above, the latest drawn, where the composition really works. This is an example of Petit's willingness to record reality without feeling the need to vary the scene, as many professional artists did. Instead he finds the angle to capture the scene best.

Sadly preservation of the monuments does not seem to have been made a condition of development, and now nothing prevents further ruin.

It is possible to approach the group from the centre of the village walking up to and behind the church, and also to walk along the stream, or river, Blithe, just a little further down the road.

When you are ready to leave Hamstall Ridware to move on to the next stop, do not follow the main road round to the left, but take the right fork.

MAVESYN RIDWARE, HIGH BRIDGE, B5014, RUGELEY WS15 4EB

The next site is only a couple of miles as the crow flies, but further without a helicopter, and if your satnav is old the map may be helpful.

Understandably Petit focused principally on the architecture of buildings, but he was also well aware of the importance of other man-made structures, especially bridges. In our day major bridges get a lot of attention – think of those on the Forth, the Tyne, and the Dartmouth crossing of the Thames, all of which have plenty of character. But there are many other more humble bridges on which our roads depend.

The High Bridge at Mavesyn Ridware used to be an important north–south link. The Trent, wide and shallow, was a major obstacle on many national routes, cutting across the centre of the country. There were several crossings, but few as essential as this.

Park the car where indicated on the map and walk onto the iron bridge walkway and, with this picture, you can see three generations of bridge. The stone one in the picture was built only a hundred years previously in the 1720s, replacing a wooden structure. Its arches and piers were attractive. However, it was not well maintained, as we sometimes find with our roads today. The structure has split in the middle and trees are growing out of it. Rather than repair they replaced it, just to the west, between 1829 and 1832 with the iron structure you are on, at the time the biggest span of any in the country and now given preservation status. The modern bridge was added only in 1996.

1.4e. High Bridges, near Mavesyn Ridware, 1830s, 19 × 27. The crumbling state of the old bridge, with trees growing on it, is confirmed by other drawings of it at the time.

1.5a. Old Church, Rugeley, c. 1835, 14 × 20. A small picture from the same dark monochrome album as Tixall.

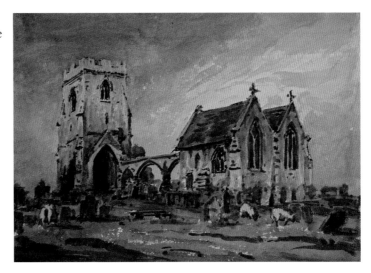

There was a small battle between Mavesyn Ridware and Handsacre folk just by the bridge in 1403, apparently the culmination of a long feud and sparked by the mini-civil war between Henry IV and Percy. In true Shakespearian fashion, the next generation of the Mavesyns and Handsacres married and overcame the feud. Another two significant bridges feature at Burton-on-Trent, tour 3, and at Sandon, tour 5.

1.5. RUGELEY OLD CHURCH, STATION ROAD, RUGELEY, WS15 2AB

Head back west to Rugeley which can be reached in ten minutes and five miles. The old St Augustine's church is opposite the new and parking can be found on the verge on the 'new' side of the road.

Rugeley is a small town on the edge of Cannock Chase area of outstanding natural beauty. In Petit's day Rugeley was described as 'the handsomest market town in the region' with especially numerous (about thirty) hatters. On the Trent, and the canal, Rugeley had six coal and iron work-

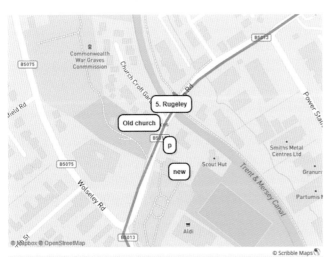

ings. A large-scale mine and the prominent power station opened in the 1960s, and the hatters have all disappeared.

The graveyard of the new St Augustine's contains the victims of two grisly murders, one in 1839 and one in 1855, that took Rugeley briefly to national notoriety.

The old church sits in a small park with a plaque that explains some of its history. The original church was built in the twelfth century and the tower added in the fourteenth. The new church across the road was built in the

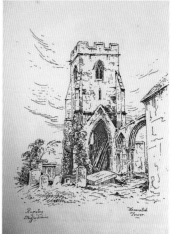

1.5b. The Tower, Old Church, Rugeley, c. 1843, 32 × 24. Much later than fig. 1.5a, this was used as an illustration in Petit's second book, *Remarks on Architectural Character*.

1.5c. The Tower, Old Church, Rugeley, illustration XXIX (29) in *Remarks on Architectural Character* (1845).

nineteenth century when the old one became too small. You will not find the sheep from Petit's picture. Apart from the tower it is a slightly diminished sight besides the busy road, but the tower is still impressive. The first, smaller picture is from the 1835 album that includes the Tixall gatehouse. He then returned to draw just the tower in about 1843, to include in his second book, *Remarks on Architectural Character* (1845). The book illustration is shown alongside the painting.

This is a good moment to explain a bit more about architectural character. The Ecclesiological Society was founded in 1841, around the time that Petit's first book came out, and their journal began in 1842. Its members aggressively advocated only one particular Gothic, English late thirteenth- to fourteenth-century, often called Decorated,[1] and were to become influential for a while. They lambasted Petit and all that he stood for: that there is beauty in every style, including foreign

---

1. Gothic is not considered to be a single style, but one that evolved through different phases, each with its own peculiarities, names and (overlapping) periods. Simplistically: Early English (1180–1270), Decorated (1270–1370) and Perpendicular (1370–1520).

examples, that all should be preserved; and that new buildings should strive for originality rather than copy-Gothic. They also ridiculed the idea that 'mere' beauty had a place in religious architecture. In his second book Petit, perhaps a little defensively, explains that it is more than just beauty which he wants to preserve, and wants architects to strive for – hence the introduction of Character.

In his words: '[the architect] will take care that his work shall be, and shall appear to be, firm and lasting; such ornament as he is able to use he will consider wholly subordinate … He will not be so anxious to produce a picturesque effect, or to imitate a particular style, as to design what shall be seen and felt to be a good church. If he is earnest, his work will not be deficient in character.'

This applied not just to churches: 'A real Swiss cottage is as characteristic as it is picturesque … can the same character be given to the best imitation of a Swiss cottage?' and 'More architectural character is destroyed by additions than by dilapidation … by depriving us of our associations …'

For Petit Rugeley demonstrated character. It is, a great example of a perfectly proportioned tower without a spire, and as such it was not acceptable to the Gothicists (albeit of the right century). Compare the character on each side of the road. No expertise needed, just gut feeling.

We will see other examples of preservation and alteration of architectural character throughout all tours, especially in the more southerly ones.

1.6. On Cannock Chase, WS15 1QR

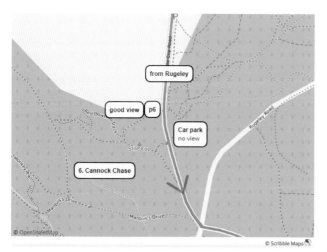

Next some landscape. Exit Rugeley on the A460 Hednesford Road and you quickly enter Cannock Chase. It is the largest surviving lowland heath in the Midlands, and, with its own charm and beauty, quite distinct from hillier British countryside.

At the time of the Domesday book it was scarcely populated because its sandy soils were too poor for farming. It was an oak forest reserved for hunting. In 1290 King Edward I turned it over to the Bishop of Lichfield. In the years leading up to the industrial revolution increasing demand for charcoal led to steady deforestation, which was not systematically reversed until replanting in the 1920s.

Petit's three pictures shown here are supposedly after deforestation although they show some tree cover was still left. The first is from the 1830s when Petit took care in finishing landscapes, and is starting to find his own style, which is unique to him and his circle, in terms of creating visual impressions which convey the drama of a scene.

A couple of miles out of Rugeley, find your way to Stile Cop Road. The postcode is for Stile Cop car park, but here new growth obscures the views to most directions except the north east. Far better is to return 100 metres north to an opening on the left and walk a little way along that path. There one can see Petit's view, with similar trees to boot.

1.6a. On Cannock Chase, 1830s, 32 x 23. An early landscape, showing aspects of the drama and emotion that Petit would gradually become proficient in communicating.

The gossipy diarist Augustus Hare recorded a picnic party on Cannock Chase with Petit's niece, Sarah Salt, with whom he was staying at Weeping Cross, on the outskirts of Stafford:

> a wild healthy upland, with groups of old firs and oaks, extending unenclosed for 15 miles and surrounded by noblemen's houses and parks. Here we joined a picnic party of fifty people. English fashion, scarcely anybody spoke to anybody else…

Hare seemed to spend his life visiting gentry all over the country and in Europe, during the Victorian era. He made the acquaintance of Petit, his sister Emma and niece, Sarah, in France in 1861 and then visited first Sarah and then Petit in August 1862. We will encounter Hare again in tour 8.

MYSTERY PICTURE(S) – On Cannock Chase. Because of the uncertainty in their locations, all but aficionados of Cannock Chase should proceed to Upper Longdon, 1.8 below.

The next picture appears to be taken near one of those big estates, Beaudesert Hall, the country seat of the Bishop of Lichfield, and now a Scout Camp and Outdoor Activity Centre. The address is ws15 4JJ, but you must phone ahead

1.6b. On Cannock Chase, 1843, approx 26 × 34. Looking towards the back of an estate, possibly Beaudesert Hall

1.6c. On Cannock Chase, 1843, 22 × 28. Unknown location in Cannock Chase, with a strange tree-less mound at right

to get permission to visit, and this is mainly granted early in the week, rather than Friday to Sunday when the camp is busy.

The hall is a complete ruin with the jungle starting to take it back, a very unusual sight in the UK. The picture would appear to be taken from the back of the old hall, the opposite side from which one approaches along the old avenue, and looking back to the ruin, but this is by no means certain.

The last picture is completely unknown although the small tree-less hill to the right might be recognisable. Cannock Chase is unusual with many beautiful parts, however it is a landscape that has been subject to huge human influence, several times over the centuries. Now evergreen, as well as deciduous, planting is altering the character of the landscape again and blocking some of the ancient views, presumably according to some design which is not obvious to me.

From the early 1840s Petit's pictures started to become rougher, with reddish skies. His intention was to capture the effect impressionistically, and more economically (to save his own time and logistics), using fewer colours. These two pictures probably date from 1843 and demonstrate this short period in the evolution in his style

While the southern tours are mostly architecture, tours 6 and 7, to the north, are mostly landscapes. There we will see much less human impact than in Cannock Chase.

1.7. Upper Longdon, The Grange, Upper Way, WS15 1PG

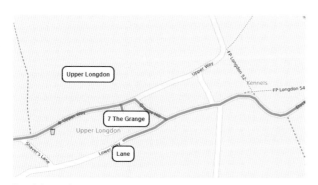

Upper Longdon is only a mile or so from Stile Cop, straight across the crossroads one comes to going south east. The Grange is now a well-to-do housing development, nothing like the pictures shown – the history is interesting, but the building on the next page has gone.

Petit bought land on what was then 'Longdon Ridge, Rugeley' and commenced building his summer house in 1855. He painted these pictures of the building in progress in November of that year. It was a remarkable building, consisting of just 4 large rooms on one floor,

1.7a. Bumblekyte, 1855, 24 × 32. View to the south east, showing Lichfield spires in the distance. These can indeed just be seen from the location

1.7b. Bumblekyte, 1855, 24 × 32. View from the south east, on the edge of a sharp drop down to the lane below.

with a roof terrace. Its design was exhibited at the Architectural Exhibition (an annual shindig held in Conduit Street, London, each year with large exhibitions and public lectures) of 1856, and demonstrated exactly the originality that he had been calling for. He called it Bumblekyte – local slang for blackberry brambles. Later it became The Brambles.

After his sister's death in 1893 the house was sold to a local landowner named Forster, who made it a more conventional two-storey house which he called the Grange.[2] This was then torn down to make room for the fifteen houses that you now see. The land at the back slopes steeply down and it is possible to see the spires of Lichfield from the back patios of some houses, as in the picture, middle right.

This was one of just two buildings that Petit designed, the other is a chapel at Caerdeon in North Wales, which fortunately still survives and has been granted Grade I protection (see page 169 and fig. 9.13). Besides these, Petit also designed some tracery work in St Paul's cathedral, when new windows were being installed.

2. The mystery of what had become of Bumblekyte, and the location of the landscapes below, was unravelled by Gareth Evans and his family, residents of the Grange.

1.7c. Near Bumblekyte, 1867, 38 × 28. Believed to be the lane below the house, in Petit's late impressionist style.

1.7d. Near Bumblekyte, 1867, 38 × 28. Similar to the above but with a person who may well be his sister sitting in view. Emma was his main support during his career.

As pictures these are just typical architectural sketches which he would have done while supervising construction. Here it is the unusual design of the building that is interesting. Character by the bucketful. Petit summed up his opinion on architecture thus:

> In any case, whether we revive or invent anew, let us aim to go beyond our predecessors, let us aim at some standard of perfection above any which they reached … I may be describing an impossibility; but if we try to reach it, we shall be sure to do something.

Towards the end of his life Petit painted numerous pictures around here on his frequent stays, as did his sisters. The two shown are of the lane beneath the Grange/Bumblekyte, drawn in 1867.

'Visible brush strokes to convey the impressions of the subject; capturing the effects of light; en plein air' are essential aspects of Impressionism which was just coalescing at the same time – the mid-1860s – in Paris. Petit probably would have been aware of this, and seems to have been experimenting with similar techniques 'striving to reach a new standard'.

Among the charming things about Petit are the doodles on the backs of his later pictures. Augustus Hare, whom we met at Cannock Chase, remarked on it as being part of his obsessive

1.7e. Drawing on the back of 1.7c. Most of Petit's later pictures carry these cartoons, recording the events of the day.

1.7f. Drawing on the back of 1.7d. Petit and his sister Emma are always recognizable, he by his waistcoat and she by the umbrella – vital in enabling him to continue drawing whatever the weather.

activity. They record events of the day. Shown on the back of the left-hand watercolour is a typical series of small incidents, including what might be his sister Emma knocking him off his sketching stool; and on the right a family party, with his sister seemingly collapsed on the floor.

I wonder if that is Emma sitting by the side of the path in the second watercolour on the previous page. She worked closely with him from around 1845 on, organising his albums, and often painting alongside him. After his death she arranged for the publication of three posthumous articles by Petit, as well as his long, unfinished poem, 'The Greater and Lesser Light' where he attempts a reconciliation of religious belief with scientific rationality. I include a few sample verses when we are in the beautiful valleys of Dovedale (tour 7).

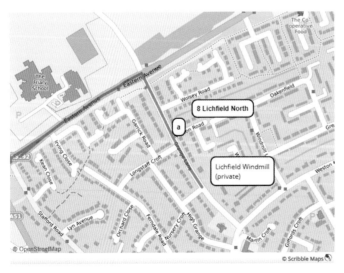

1.8 Grange Lane, North Lichfield, ws13 7ed

The tour finishes on the outskirts of Lichfield. Although there is a Windmill Lane behind it, the old windmill was on Grange Lane opposite the entry to the road called Little Grange. Now Windmill House is an interesting, grade II-listed, private house. The spires of the cathedral are visible from further up Grange Lane where the artist must have sat.

36

1.8. Lichfield, c. 1857, 27 × 37. Courtesy of the Samuel Johnson Birthplace Museum, Lichfield. View from the north. Whenever at home in Lichfield Petit would draw the Cathedral, and these are some of his most-finished watercolours.

Petit's home was in Lichfield from 1823 on, apart from a brief spell working as a curate in Essex until 1834, and then living in Shifnal until the mid-1840s. He spent several months each year here, even when he also had a home in Lincoln's Inn, London, inherited from his uncle, and travelled for much of the time. And, when he was in Lichfield he often painted views of the cathedral. Tour 8 is a walking tour of the town that takes in lots of examples.

However many of Petit's pictures have secondary reasons for being drawn too. In this case, as you see, the mill, which powered a local brickworks, is still a windmill. Apparently it reopened in 1857 having been converted to steam (i.e. no longer a windmill). It would be absolutely typical of Petit to make his painting before it was lost. Much art is of course done for posterity in one way or another; Petit's message to us is more than just topography in the sense of showing what was where at a particular time, which can be dull. He often combines this 'reporting' with capturing the feeling of the scene, what he called its 'effect'; one reason why his art was so popular in his time.

2.1a. St Mary's, Stafford, from the south west. c. 1835, 19 × 25. Petit painted this church frequently leading up to its restoration in 1843, and showing works underway. This appears to have been made a few years earlier.

Tour 2

Stafford to Stoke: Battles with Gothicists

This tour starts with a walk around the centre of Stafford, and then heads west and north ending on the outskirts of Stoke. It could be done in two halves, Stafford, and the rest. There is more of a focus on Petit's battles with the Gothicists in this tour because of the significance of this at St Mary's, the main church in Stafford which Petit fought to protect. Because of this battle Petit painted St Mary's from all around Stafford so we get a good appreciation of how the town has changed.

This chapter also includes Cheadle, the only location of a place in this book which Petit did not paint. Augustus Pugin was the inspiration for the most important subsequent Gothic architects and their advocates in the middle and late Victorian age. Gilbert Scott and the Ecclesiologists often acknowledged their debt to him, and in Cheadle is one of his best surviving buildings. There you

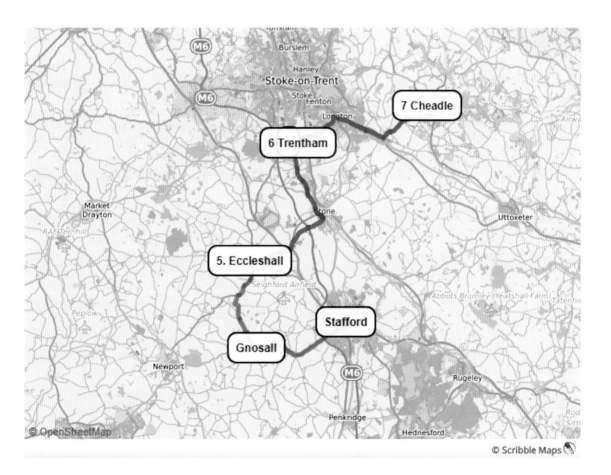

© Scribble Maps

can see what some describe as the finest example of Victorian Gothic – both what makes it extraordinary and full of character, and also why Petit was right to oppose dogmatic rules for all new builds and restorations.

First to Stafford.

It is something to have a county town and a city so rich in history as Stafford and Lichfield so close together. While Lichfield was the religious capital of a huge diocese, Stafford became the military and commercial centre for the region before the Norman Conquest, and a key fortification (called 'burh'), from which the heirs of Alfred the Great continued their father's efforts to unify England.

Later, it naturally evolved to the county town and one of the most important Norman earldoms, based around the castle. Although it has to be said that rather a large number of Earls of Stafford managed to get themselves executed – four I believe. Having just about survived proximity to the M6, soon it will be sandwiched between that and the HS2 rail line, if the proposed route is carried out, despite sterling opposition from the Stafford Borough Council.

The first three groups of pictures are all in Stafford and can make a very pleasant circular walk – the windmill and other pictures are at opposite ends of Victoria Park along the River Sow, with St Mary's overlooking both. Park at any of the central car parks, the easiest I have found is right by the windmill at ST16 2QB, marked P on the map, where you will end up. But best start the tour at point 1.

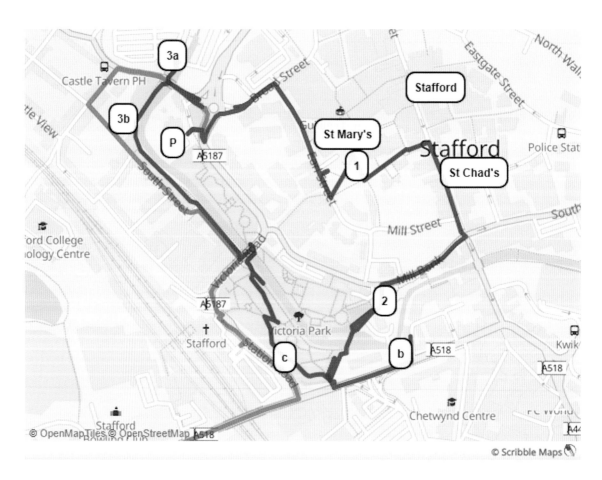

© Scribble Maps

2.1 St Mary's Stafford, st16 2ap

As the most important church of an important town, St Mary's itself has had an eventful history, passing between the crown and the Earls of Stafford, or being a semi-independent college. For us, it became the focus of a significant conflict early in their careers between Petit and George Gilbert Scott, who won the commission to restore the church in 1841.

Neither men had a fraction of the fame or authority they would later go on to acquire. Petit had just written his first book which came out in March of that year. It was very well received and this gave him some sway, but not nearly as much as he had later on. Scott was a popular young architect, specializing in churches, who had been smitten by Augustus Pugin's passion for middle Gothic. Later he was to become one of the most celebrated architects of the Victorian age, handling railway stations, government buildings and the restoration of twenty-five cathedrals – a large majority – as well as countless churches.

The crux of their argument was whether to re-build the south transept

2.1b. St Mary's, Stafford, 30 × 22, c. 1842, the South Transept before restoration began, altogether more optimistic in mood

with a sloping, proper Gothic roof or leave it flattish. If you stand back from the south-west corner of the church, roughly in line with the 'Soup Kitchen', and compare what you can see with the first two of these pictures (2.1a and 2.1b) you will understand the debate. To my mind, while the church is of course still very beautiful, something has been diminished compared to the picture. Character. Game and set, Petit – the flat roof did not need changing. But look again and you will see that being right is not the same as winning. The match went to Scott and the sloping-roof brigade got their way.

Petit was fighting against the tide of fashion for Gothic. Scott's argument was that the original roof had been sloping until the spire collapsed in the sixteenth century. As ever, the finer details of the argument did not matter, he won by persuading the local committee to put the debate in front of wholly prejudiced judges – the Oxford Architectural and Cambridge Ecclesiological Societies.

Does it matter now? Later Scott himself admitted that this small incident had a major influence on the debate about how to do restoration, which he and everyone eventually agreed should be

2.1c. St Mary's, Stafford, c. 1843, 23 × 29. From the south. Just after restoration began.

minimal, as Petit had argued. So Petit's labours, including the many pictures shown here, were not wasted.

Most good citizens of Stafford presumably do not notice, and know nothing of what might have been. But in a sense that is the point about architecture, you have to live with the decision for a very long time. Those with the inclination to take an interest do an enormous service to their communities, even more so now than in the past when it was more common to do so.

This view is also a reminder of Petit's admirable behavior, despite losing a battle. He never gave up presenting his point of view for the next twenty-seven years, doggedly and persistently, but always rationally and politely, despite numerous personal provocations, and eventually the tide turned. Scott was not always so gentlemanly and would stop at nothing to promote himself. Though usually very respectful to Petit, in a public exchange of letters in 1856 he was not above resorting to unpleasant personal slights on Petit and a friend in order to try to maintain his position.

Gradually the dogma weakened and by the 1850s Scott tired of the Ecclesiologists because they kept changing their mind as to what was the 'correct' version of Gothic. By the end of his life, in his memoirs, he claimed to have always supported the case for maximum preservation; that Petit

2.1b. The font, c. 1843, 18 × 18. The Ian Cooke Collection. Amid the rubble of the restoration.

was a wonderful man and a great artist; and he expressed a wish that they had been closer, despite Petit's 'errors' in matters architectural. Taking all their interactions together, I think he possibly meant it.

So, this church is the scene of the first significant battle to establish historic building protection, an issue we will see elsewhere. If ever there is a will among the good citizens of Stafford to return the south transept to its previous state, I will donate to the cause. After finding the other pictures, if you wish, leave the square via the south east alley and turn right along the pedestrianized Greengate St, a few yards along is St Chads.

2.2 St Chad's and the River Sow, st16 2hp

St Chad's is also a very old church, but I am only aware of this one picture of it by Petit, drawn just as its restoration was getting underway – in contrast to about twenty of St Mary's, which he painted inside and out before its restoration, partly to demonstrate its visual significance in making his arguments. It is extraordinary to have two old churches quite so close together. St Chad's was one of the smallest, and therefore poorest parishes in the diocese. At the time of the 1834 *History, Gazetteer and Directory of Staffordshire* it was said to contain just thirty-five of the 1,300 houses in Stafford. It had to sell four of its five bells and the walls had been cement covered in the eighteenth century to keep going. So probably it was not so attractive in Petit's day, which may explain why he may have only painted it once just before restoration. Notice the absence of pinnacles on the castle-like tower, and the single pinnacle that now stands as a monument in front of the church.

The following pictures were all done by Petit to show the character of St Mary's from various angles before it was to be altered, probably as part of his argument not to change it. They are all trickier to find than it might appear.

2.2. St Chad's, Stafford, during restoration, 26 × 36, courtesy of the Staffordshire and Stoke on Trent Archive Service (Doc D5713/2). Taken from the north, this demonstrates the extent of changes made by comparison with the present.

2.2a. St Mary's, c. 1835, 24 × 29. From the old mill on the River Stour.

From St Chad's continue along Greengate St, turning right down Millbank to the old water mill (2 on map). Judging by the view of St Mary's (facing the south transept) the first picture was drawn here. There is a plaque explaining about the mills on the site. The picture might be from before the Mill built by George Brewster, since the mill is not visible. However, according to the plaque, the mill was built by 1834, and the picture appears to be later than that (so in this I might be mistaken). Another possibility is that the mill was being rebuilt in the early 1840s to install the new wheels in 1845, also mentioned on the plaque.

The second picture shows St Chad's to the right of St Mary's, with a stretch of river heading towards the two churches. It appears to be drawn from further back than the previous picture, at the end of the small stretch of river which points towards town instead of around it. I think the exact spot is at the back of the pizzeria accessed between it and the Peugeot dealership on Newport Road, not highly recommended because it is where the bins are (b on map). Also the angles are not quite right, implying that the banks may well have been altered. The third picture (p. 46) was taken from behind the bandstand in Victoria Park, possibly on the bank near the road to the left (c on map). Only the top of St Mary's is visible. Though the pictures are all well done, this is one group where the

2.2b. St Mary's c. 1835, From Newport Road, approx 25 × 30. Courtesy of Staffordshire County Museum Service.

landscape of the present outdoes the past. The river in Petit's day was far from clean, being a sewer for the town. Piped water was introduced before sewage systems caught up, and Victoria Park had not been built. Much pleasanter now, even at the back of the pizzeria.

2.3 The Stafford Windmill (Broad Eye) Castle Hill Stafford, st16 2qb

Next walk through Victoria and then Castle Park along the river. The windmill without the arms still stands on the river edge, looking a little forlorn by comparison with the pictures. There are plans for a museum, not yet come to fruition.

If you walk past the windmill, over the bridge and turn left on the footpath, the first picture was drawn along the river bank, back towards the park, near the bench, although the view of St Mary's is now blocked by buildings which do not enhance the view. The second was drawn from the supermarket overflow car park (3b on map). The exact angle of the mill and church can be found if the church view is not blocked by trees in leaf.

2.2c. St Mary's, c. 1835. From Station Road/Victoria park, approx 18 × 35. Courtesy of Staffordshire County Museum Service.

2.3a. Broad Eye Windmill, 1830s, 30 × 23. Likely earlier than the previous picture. From the footpath across the river. The view is now blocked, however.

At the time of the 1834 Staffordshire *Gazetteer* there were two mills in Stafford referred to as the watermill and the windmill. The windmill was run by a Thomas Twigg. In 1835 a steam engine was added to maintain production when the wind was not blowing. The pictures do not show disrepair, as I first thought, but a form of sail rigging known as 'sword point' which could be variably deployed and stop the mill running too fast if the strength of wind altered. Broadeye was used as both wind and steam mill for some time. According to the Friends of Broadeye Mill's site,

2.3b. Broad Eye Windmill, c. 1835, approx 28 × 33. Courtesy of Staffordshire County Museum Service. From the Sainsbury's overflow car park. The windmill tower stands, but is currently empty.

the sails were not dismantled until the end of the century. All these pictures were painted before St Mary's was altered. As with all altered churches, there is no record of Petit painting it after its new appearance was unveiled.

Now we take to the road, first to visit two churches to the west of Stafford and then Trentham park.

2.4 Gnosall Church, Selman Street, Gnosall, st20 0er

Gnosall is an ancient village 7 miles west of Stafford, just off the A518 heading towards Newport.

The first of these pictures was drawn from the south west of the church. One can find the right angle along the lane beside the private nursery, but not the right distance, because of the new buildings along the main road. The picture could well have been done from the road.

2.4a. Gnosall Church, c. 1835, approx 20 × 30. Courtesy of Staffordshire County Museum Service. From the south west when the village was much smaller.

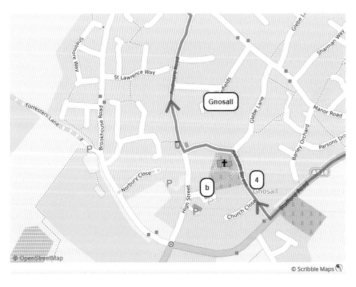

The second was drawn from the south east and shows the church before a sloping roof was put on the chancel (eastern end). Again one can find the angle but not the distance. It seems to have been done from the garden of the beautiful old rectory opposite, which one can look into from the end of Sellman Street. In the painting one can see the marks on the tower showing that a sloping roof once existed, and this provided a strong argument for the restorers to put it back. Fortunately the nave (western) roof was unaltered, and

2.4b. Gnosall Church, c. 1841, 30 × 25, The Ian Cooke Collection. From the south east, also already outside the village, judging by the cow.

from the west especially the church looks as good as before the changes.

Besides the architectural arguments, these are wonderful pictures of the village as it was, showing the central role of the church at that time.

One of the striking aspects of the church at Gnosall today is that Catholic services also take place within this Anglican church. Given that all medieval churches started off as Catholic anyway, this seems to me remarkably sensible, and yet I have only seen it rarely while chasing around those that Petit painted. Catholics often have to make do with less attractive places of worship.

2.5 Holy Trinity Church, Eccleshall, Church Street, st21 6by

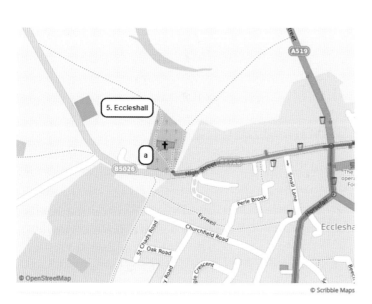

Eccleshall is a village six miles north of Gnosall, about fifteen minutes drive away. The church was completed in medieval times, but renovated in 1860 by Street, who had undertaken some of his training with George Gilbert Scott. In fact, in the opinion of many besides myself, generally, he was a more careful architect, albeit one favouring Gothic. However, in the case of this picture I think we see some loss of character.

The picture is also in the Staffordshire County collection.

2.5. Eccleshall Church, c. 1835, approx 29 × 27. Courtesy of Staffordshire County Museum Service. This picture shows that the history of the church may not be fully correct in some sources.

Again the angle can be located, but the exact spot a little back from the church I could not find, at least not with any view.

There are some unusual aspects to this church, and the changes it went through. Both some local literature and Wikipedia claim that the battlements and pinnacles on the tower were added in the early twentieth century. But as we see in Petit's picture there were more pinnacles in the 1830s. These are correctly described in the history inside the church as having been reduced and taken down during the renovation and put back later.

2.6 Trentham Hall, Stone Road, Stoke-on-Trent, ST4 8JG

Trentham is fifteen minutes north, along the A34, which has more speed cameras in five miles than anywhere else I have experienced.

You need to enter by the main (northern) gate which also leads to the retail centre. There is a charge of £9 per adult to enter the park and I paid it reluctantly, thinking it a lot for half an hour, and likely I would not include the location, but in the end I have no hesitation in recommending it. The park today is beautiful and the picture makes a very worthwhile comparison by showing what it was like in the first half of the nineteenth century before being redesigned. After entry go to the head of

2.6. Trentham, c. 1835, approx 18 × 34. Courtesy of Staffordshire County Museum Service. The picture shows the lake as built by Capability Brown, before grander changes subsequently commissioned by the then Duke, and the monument just in the process of being built.

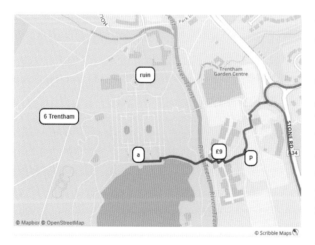

the lake and look left towards the monument to the first Duke of Sutherland.

This picture dates from just after the start of construction, and shows the wonderful gardens designed during the previous century by Capability Brown, now completely transformed. In the middle distance one can see the platform for the monument being created. I suspect Petit came here on purpose at that time to capture the scene before it was altered.

The park is now recovered from a complete wreck. The history of the house, its rapid ascent, massive expansion in the nineteenth-century, and ruin in the early twentieth century well illustrates the consequences of excessive pride. The Dukes of Sutherland built the grandest of palaces, designed by Sir Charles Barry between 1833 and 1850. Barry was the architect (with Pugin) of the Houses of Parliament. At the end of the lake, the second Duke ordered the largest statue to one's forebears in the country; they even diverted the river Trent to supplement the private lake within the park. Capability Brown's original landscape design seemed not grand enough to satisfy their pretension. Thankfully we have the picture to compare.

However, with the advent of piped water in the 1870s and 1880s, the fast growing potteries used the Trent to dump their waste and sewage and this ruined the estate. By the early twentieth century the then Duke offered the estate free to the newly formed federation of pottery towns, Stoke-on-Trent. When they rejected the offer, he himself destroyed the palace. It continued as a (smelly) ruin until improvements in water and sewage treatment by the water board in the 1950s and 60s. The nearby sewage works which the Duke first built to try to alleviate the problem are just off the map to the right.

Petit painted a few big houses in Staffordshire (see Ingestre 1.3, and Wootton Hall below, 5.8) when he was a young man. But unlike professional artists, he had not received a commission from the owners to adorn their walls. Petit never had any interest in the houses or their grandiose-ness specifically, but in seeing things as they were in their setting. When in Yorkshire in 1845 he journeyed to draw the ruin of Slingsby Castle, but seems to have ignored the far grander Castle Howard only a mile or two away which had less architectural significance for him. At least to date I am not aware of a Petit of Castle Howard. Later, on his journeys abroad, castles and houses rarely figure among the thousands of churches, ruins and landscapes.

In total these tours take us to four major estates in Staffordshire: Trentham, Ingestre, Alton and Wootton, as well as several smaller ones. At the end we will be able to judge which has fared best after 170 years.

2.7 Mystery Picture: near Cheadle

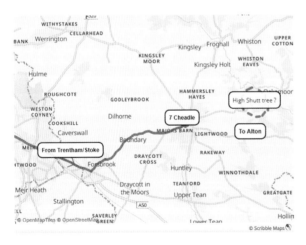

This picture must have been drawn somewhere in the beautiful hills between Alton and Cheadle, part of the 'Staffordshire Moorlands'. The two roads leading back from Alton are the B5032 through Threapwood, and the B5417 through Oakmoor. The ridge overlooking Cheadle continues to the north and south, and there is a nice small road from Threapwood to Oakmoor. There is one famous landmark around here, High Shutt, a hill with a tree at the summit that was reputed to have strange powers. But in most, not necessarily accurate, pictures of that place the tree is much more prominent than the rock, unlike in this watercolour. It is possible that somewhere the unusual rock formation seen here still exists as shown.

On the way here it is worth making an additional stop at St Giles Catholic Church, Cheadle, ST10 1ED. This detour can also be done after tour 5 from Alton and Wootton, but it fits in this tour after our introduction to the battles of architectural styles in Stafford, and visits to Gnossall and Eccleshall.

2.7. Near Cheadle, 1830s, 13 × 17. Possibly High Shutt, with a strange tree growing out of the rock.

Cheadle is home to what is often considered the best church built by Pugin and one of the finest churches built during the entire Neo-Gothic period. Pugin was the key inspiration and driving force behind the craze for Gothic, as we have said. While Petit opposed the dogmas of the Neo-Gothic movement in general, and especially for restorations, he never criticized Pugin's work and occasionally he went so far as to quote Pugin back to the Gothicists, to demonstrate that they were going far beyond their acknowledged source in their strictures. He did not paint this church so far as I am aware, so we do not have a watercolour to show of it, although he did very occasionally paint a modern gothic church.

At Cheadle, the Earl of Shrewsbury (the one from Alton Towers, of whom we learn more in tour 5) gave Pugin an unlimited budget to build a church. It is well worth seeing what the fuss is about. The town itself was considered a quaint market centre, a parish of four thousand, in 1831. Subsequently, a couple of coal mines, a brass foundry and several mills made it a small industrial centre, so quaint it certainly is not now.

Pugin's St Giles is not to be confused with the Anglican church in Cheadle which is also dedicated to St Giles. All the other churches in these pictures and tours are medieval, but this was built from scratch and opened in 1846. It was already famous before it was completed and the opening attracted Catholic bigwigs from all over Europe, presumably staying as guests of the Earl.

Those who have either completed these tours, or already know much about the battle of styles in architecture, will not need any explanation. But for those for whom all this is still new, some comments might be helpful.

The interior is quite extraordinary and deservedly makes this church one of the most interesting in the country. The tiles and other interior design features echo the Houses of Parliament and are Pugin's own invention, much more than fourteenth-century Gothic. The exterior boasts a great spire, and the whole harmonizes with the school and related buildings close by, which Pugin also designed. Overall the exterior is just a bit more elaborate than the many other Victorian Gothic churches which repeat endlessly across Britain, or the mock-Gothic restorations which disfigured medieval churches. Its exterior would be more impressive if we were not over-familiar with the basic style.

Cheadle is beautiful precisely because it is more than a copy of a Gothic church. I think Petit was absolutely right to oppose Pugin's and the Gothicists' views as hard and fast rules for everyone, everywhere. This debate does not just relate to churches. The lesson applies equally to our shopping centres, schools and hospitals. As Petit said about a copy: 'the highest praise is that a thing may be taken for something it is not.'

Tour 3

From Lichfield East: Snow, Pigeons and Symmetry

This tour starts with three 'snow' pictures all painted in February 1855 on the outskirts of Lichfield (another unidentified one is in the Introduction), before returning to earlier pictures in an arc to the East. The total travel time is around one hour.

This is a flattish region, which might at first sight not appear too interesting, but it contains a loop of the River Trent as it turns back north after heading south, and some beautiful villages making use of every clump of higher ground in the area. The canal network first intruded, and then, in Petit's day the train lines were built. Now HS2 is about to inflict further damage on this unusual landscape as it goes around Lichfield. The second and third points on this tour may become impossible to visit if phase 2 does go ahead.

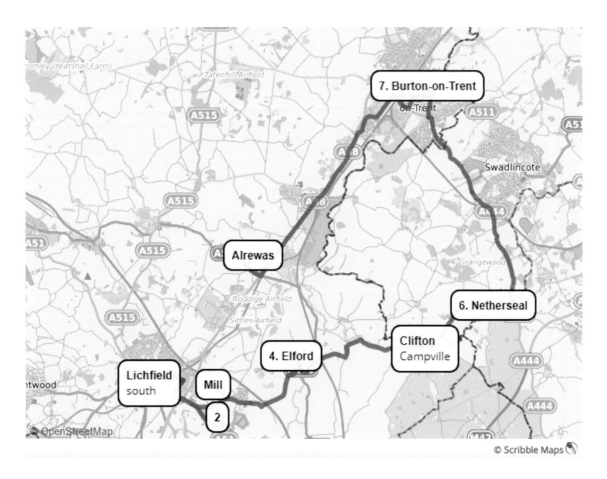

3.1. Lichfield, 1855, 26 × 37. From the southern approach, possibly along the old Roman Way. St Michael's is shown to the left of the Cathedral.

3.1 Lichfield from the South, ws14 9aw – Snow 20 February 1855

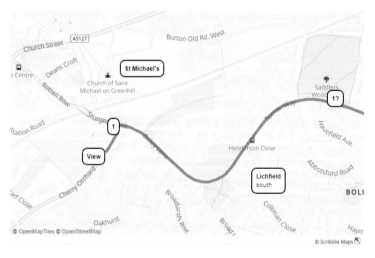

This watercolour was made, I believe, somewhere along the Roman Way leading out of Lichfield towards the Tamworth Road, with St Michael's on an elevated point to the left. Probably it was just before the left-hand bend in the road seen also in the picture, because there is a good chance the road has not changed. Now one can see the cathedral at the right angle at the junction of Cherry Orchard and Sturgeon's

Hill. This is a beautiful viewpoint, but too close in, with St Mary's standing in for St Michael's, which here is just to the right. From further away, the view seems to be blocked (at least I have not found a spot).

The thing about this whole sequence of pictures is of course the snow. Winters were particularly bad in Victorian times – a mini ice age, frozen rivers etc., which we cannot remember – and we have almost no record of what it looked like, especially in ordinary places.

Conventional artists rarely painted snow scenes, in England at least. They were not commercial. Possibly no one wanted to be reminded of such unpleasantness, so patrons did not ask for them. Moreover, artists did not want to sketch in the freezing cold, which is nothing like the experience of painting a balmy summer woodland. Lastly, capturing the effect of snow in watercolour is technically quite difficult. I think Petit conveys it very well, by the way, but you can be your own judge.

In 1855 Petit, aged 54, was entering the period of his greatest renown. He had just published his third and most thoroughly researched book, *Architectural Studies in France*, which had been very well received. He was due to make several speeches to architectural societies in the coming month (Hereford two weeks after these paintings in early February and then Oxford in March) and deliver his first paper to the RIBA a little later, all railing against the limitations of Gothic. Yet he went out to paint in the snow for a week in mid-winter.

3.2 Whittington Race Course, Tamworth Road, Whittington, ws14 9pw

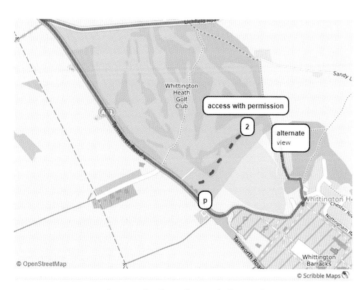

Two miles, and five minutes away, Whittington Race Course is actually now Whittington barracks and golf course. The club house, a remarkable building and worth the visit, used to house soldiers and was built towards the end of the nineteenth century, but previously it was the grandstand for the racecourse, and still looks like it.

Racing here was most popular in the eighteenth century, the grandstand was built in 1775, for one of the most well attended venues in the midlands. During the nineteenth century its popularity declined until the military acquired the land for barracks to house a militia battalion, some twenty years after this was painted.

Made on 7 February 1855, my first guess was that the picture was drawn from the grandstand (which I believe was still in use then) looking towards the village of Whittington, where the church of St Giles can be seen. But the correct spot is at the end of the first hole of the golf course, where a lone tree stands next to the green – because the picture does not cover the race course itself, but only the rough ground on the other side, where the view is still similar. On a quiet day you might get

3.2. Whittington, 1855, 26 × 37. From the edge of the race course, now the end of the first fairway on the golf course, looking towards the village.

permission to walk out there, or, a little easier, is to drive round to the alternative viewpoint shown on the map above. From this point there is a footpath leading from the road from where you can look up to the green and tree and across to a similar view.

Catch this while you can. HS2 may soon drive straight through the golf course, destroying the clubhouse and five holes. The club has had to take the reinstatement provisions and will move sideways.

3.3 HUDDLESFORD MILL, CAPPERS LANE, WS14 9JW

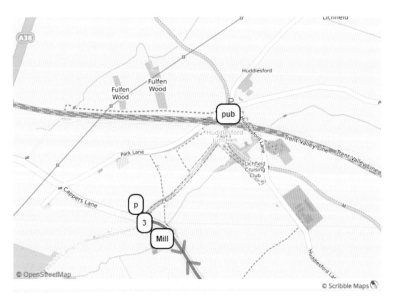

A further two miles and five minutes, the third picture in this group was made a week later, on 13 February 1855. Unfortunately it is also in the direct path of HS2.

There is a house called The Watermill at the address given, which I believe is one and the same location as Huddlesford Mill shown below. The canal was already built and well used by 1855 and although it is a more important waterway, it would not have had an old mill

3.3. Huddlesford Mill, 1855, 26 × 37. Not many people would be tempted to go out sketching in the middle of February, not once, but for several days in a row.

associated with it, whereas the stream here likely did, and one can hear the water flowing still. The Watermill is the second house back from the road and you can walk up to the gate.

In 1834 the mill here was called Bunnings Mill and run by one Thomas Capper, after whom the lane was apparently named. I think the picture was drawn from on the canal bridge.

Incidentally if you head back towards Lichfield and turn first right along the canal, you soon come to a nicely situated pub, the Plough, which has been here for several centuries. It is remarkably busy for a small village, perhaps because much of the resident population live on canal boats, and in Petit's day it was likely the same. Indeed the population of canal dwellers, bargemen, was considerably more than today. Difficult living through such winters no doubt.

3.4 ELFORD, B79 9DQ

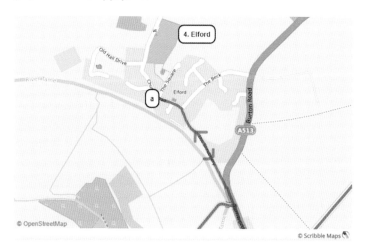

Five miles and ten minutes away is the curious village of Elford, on the banks of the river Tame. The postcode is for Church Road where will be found St Peter's, although we want the junction with The Square, in the heart of the old village and before the church.

If Petit did not paint the church, and I do not know of a picture yet, then you can be sure the church is relatively modern. And such is the

3.4. Elford, c. 1835 approx 18 × 32. Courtesy of Staffordshire County Museum Service. It seems Petit decided on a view rather than painting the church, for whatever reason.

case. Although there had been a Norman church, it had to be completely rebuilt in the late 1840s.

This picture appears to be taken along the road from a position on Church Road, at the junction with 'The Square'. Opposite is one of the oldest houses in the village, a smithy, and the picture seems to be taken looking along past the old Forge, which can still be seen at the side of the road, down towards the river, which would be visible but for other buildings. It runs close by at the back of the houses.

The picture will have been drawn in the late 1830s before the re-building of the church. The old church was in very poor condition and Petit possibly came to see if he would take a position on it. I have no record of him doing so.

Now to one of the most celebrated church buildings in the county.

3.5 Clifton Campville, Church Street, B79 0AR

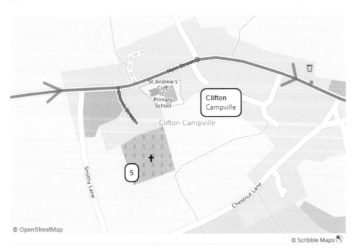

From Elford you head east only five miles and twelve minutes to the church of St Andrew, Clifton Campville. The spire is visible from Lichfield on a good day. It is said to be one of the finest parish churches in Staffordshire. Petit can help us understand why.

Here is an example of what Petit had to say about what separates the real thing from contemporary copies: 'There is a manifest propriety, a

3.5a. Clifton Campville, illustration facing p.61, vol. 2 of *Remarks on Church Architecture*, a different view from an earlier watercolour.

3.5b. Clifton Campville, c. 1844, 34 × 25. One of the finest steeples to be found in the country.

careful adjustment, and a remarkable gracefulness of composition which pervades the whole (of the body of medieval church architecture)…till this is not only felt and appreciated, but reduced to practice, little beauty will result from the imitation of details.' His first book includes three hundred of the most beautiful churches from all over the UK and Europe, including Clifton Campville.

As a western steeple exhibiting at once great beauty of outline and extreme simplicity of composition, I cannot do better than set before the reader that of Clifton in Staffordshire, about 12 miles east of Lichfield… Standing upon a slight eminence, in a rather level tract of country, it is a very conspicuous object at a considerable distance, and is, in fact, one of the principal features in the fine landscape commanded from St. Michael's churchyard in Lichfield. The boldness of the diagonal buttresses, the low position of the belfry-window, and the lofty pinnacles annexed to the spire by flying buttresses, are all accessories to its beauty.

There are two or three other fine steeples in the region, which we will see from a distance, yet this stands above the others because of the details of its composition that Petit helpfully lists.

G. E. Street, who we also met at Eccleshall in tour 2, carried out a restoration of this church in 1860. The work was not very damaging because the spire is entirely the same. However, notice that the roof of the nave is now higher against the spire than it was – that seems to be the most alterative change. Generally the original design was such that it matched the dogma of the Gothicists, and, by 1860 the dogma had advanced a long way from the 1830s and 1840s so that the rules were more respectful of what was there before. Street is also reputed to be one of the finest architects of the period – not as famous as George Gilbert Scott so less known to us now – but still I wish the old roof line had been kept, as it would make the spire even more impressive, as in Petit's picture. It was only in his second book that Petit talked explicitly about architectural character; that is not mentioned so directly by him in his first book, but that is what Street to some extent reduced.

The river is the Mease, running east to the Trent.

3.6 Netherseale and Seale, Derbyshire, Church Street, DE12 8DF

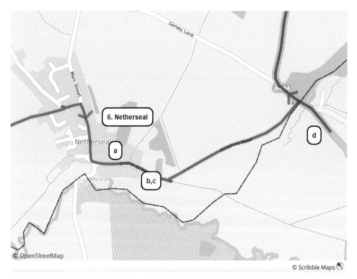

Our next Staffordshire destination is Burton on Trent, but to get there we will go on for ten minutes over the Derbyshire border to Netherseale – modern spelling Netherseal. The first picture is of the church tower, from the village green where you arrive if approaching from the west. The church was restored and the nave rebuilt in 1874, but the tower was largely untouched from when Petit painted this in about 1833.

Netherseale is deep into Gresley territory. The Gresley baronetcy, whose ancestry dated from the thirteenth century eventually died out not so long ago in the twentieth century. Petit married one Louisa Reid, whose younger sister, Georgina, married Nigel Gresley of Barton-under-Needwood in 1831. He by happenstance, i.e. some premature deaths, inherited the baronetcy, and hence the main seat at Overseale and the manor here at Netherseale, and held it until his death in 1847. We will also encounter the Gresleys in Lichfield at Gresley Row in tour 8.

The Gresleys were active antiquarians and watercolourists who were closely associated with Petit through the Anastatic Drawing Society. This curious society was founded by the Reverend John Gresley, of 'Over Seile', as opposed to Netherseal where we are now, in 1855 to draw old buildings of interest using a newly discovered method of reproduction – Anastatic printing, a precursor of photocopying – little knowing that mass photography was just around the corner. It had 150 members from the start, including ten Gresleys, all from hereabouts. They published an album each year, now

3.6a. Netherseale, c. 1834, 20 × 14. The church tower, possibly from the village green.

viewable on the internet, and Petit contributed drawings to each of their annual collections.[1]

The next two pictures show the Grade-I listed dovecote that is built into the wall of the stables of the old manor. This is further along on the right side, fifty metres after the church.

There were four sisters in the Reid family. The family was wealthy, and so highly rated in the marriage scene of the day. Harriet, the youngest, also married a baronet, the Lloyds of South Wales. She is the only one of whom I have seen a picture, in which she appears slight and attractive.

Amelia the fourth sister, who remained unmarried, was a good artist, and occasionally painted with Petit and his sisters. We will encounter her in Gloucestershire on another occasion.

---

1   After Rev Gresley died in 1865 there was a continuation for a few years by the Ilam Anastatic Drawing Society…so much earnest effort that is now just a footnote.

3.6b. Dovecote, Netherseale, c. 1831, 18 × 20. Petit painted the dovecote on several occasions, but may not have drawn the house, at least I have not found any yet. One wonders if this might have caused offence.

These pictures are certainly early, which in Petit terms means before 1832, and somewhat damaged. I suspect he might have drawn them on a visit to the Gresleys perhaps for his sister-in-law's wedding. The askew cupola will have caught his attention.

Dovecotes were built all over Britain from the fourteenth to the seventeenth centuries, when pigeons were a frequent form of communication – often shown in films of the Tudors – and food. The Netherseale one is later, from the seventeenth century. Later, in *Architectural Character*, Petit includes a picture of a different dovecote as an example of character achieved by the architect/builder just getting the job done diligently, exactly as we see here.

The fourth picture looks towards a spired church. There are several good candidates, such as Lullington, but I think it is the beautiful, but now redundant church at Stretton en le Field to the south-west, across another county border in Leicestershire. There are several possible viewpoints along the road out of Netherseale, however I think it might have been taken from the now busy A444 as it heads downhill to the bridge over the stream (see d on map).

3.6c. Dovecote, Netherseale, c. 1831, 18 × 27. Probably, but not certainly, the same, from an opposite view.

3.6d. View towards Stretton-le-Field, c. 1831, 19 × 27. Another early, more conventional landscape.

3.7a. Unnamed, possibly the Old Trent Bridge, 1830s, 19 × 27. The church shown over the bridge might be the old church dedicated to St Modwen.

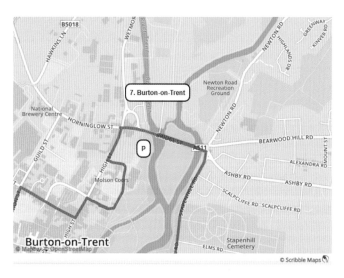

3.7 HIGH ST, BURTON-ON-TRENT DE14 1AH

Now continue north to Burton-on-Trent, another historic Staffordshire town scarcely visited from outside the region. The post code will take you to outside the library on the banks of the river.

While there are interesting churches and old breweries, it is the setting of Burton that demands most attention, so perhaps appropriate that we focus on the bridges there. The address given is a useful place to view the scale of the river with its meadow, the existing bridges, and to find parking if you have time to walk.

The bridge at Burton was always a key transport link between east and west, despite the 500 metre width that had to be spanned. Bridges are recorded from the twelfth century but no doubt there were fords and smaller bridges before then at this point. Petit's pictures show the Old Trent Bridge, described by the then County Surveyor as 'the longest, most ancient and most inconvenient structure of its kind.' It had 36 arches and snaked across the Trent just to the south of the present straight bridge that we see, which was built between 1859 and 1864.

Historically the town produced ornamental works in alabaster sourced from the nearby Needwood forest, however even by Petit's time the town was famous for its ale. In 1831, the population of Burton, including the Derbyshire side was all of 7,347, with 'nine extensive breweries sending

3.7b. On the Trent, late 1830s/early 40s, 27 × 22. This shows the eastern end of the old bridge, from the island between the streams of the river.

produce to all parts of Britain, and to many foreign countries, especially the East and West Indies'.

There are many places where a bridge is the dominant architectural structure, think the Severn, Newcastle, the Forth etc. Other artists did do romantic scenes like Waterloo Bridge at Sunset, Petit seems to haven painted them more to capture their architectural effect. At odd points in his speeches Petit refers to the classical design of Roman viaducts as well as modern Victorian bridges, and he had no qualms to make them the object of his watercolours throughout his life.

In contrast to the county surveyor, the Gazetteer William White described the bridge at Burton in 1834 as 'one of the noblest fabrics of the king in England' and 'the most entire and remarkable object of antiquity possessed by this town'. The land between the two streams was called the Island of Andressey where lived St Modwen, who cured King Alfred of some dreadful disease as a boy. She founded an abbey just downstream from here, where now there is a church built in the eighteenth century to replace the ancient structures (which maybe why we find Petits of the bridge and not of that). From the library there are footpaths both to the island and to the church.

3.8. Alrewas Church, c. 1839–42, 16 × 18. Petit will have painted this around the time of his first book, although for whatever reason it does not feature in the book itself.

3.8 ALREWAS, ALL SAINTS CHURCH, CHURCH ROAD, DE13 7BT

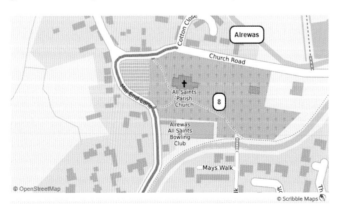

Our last stop is back towards Lichfield just off the main A38 at the curiously named and very attractively located village of Alrewas. Apparently the name derives from Old English meaning alder trees on the river plain.

Petit painted this picture in about 1839–42, and he painted the scene again in 1859 although that picture has not yet come to light. You can see a marked development of Petit's technique in this and the previous picture at Burton, by comparison with the rather conventional and perhaps less interesting pictures at Netherseal, which were done a decade earlier. As the biographical note explains, the 1830s and 1840s were a time of great variation and development of his style.

Architecturally, it is the changes to the church that are particularly interesting. The church Petit saw and drew was wonderfully, and indeed beautifully, unsymmetrical: the two buildings joined at the sides and especially the sloping and the flat roofs of each. Looking at the church as it is today it has been extended and made more symmetrical with similar shaped roofs, a restoration and extension carried out in 1877 according to church records. If the restoration had been done before the 1860s the sloping roof would have won, but here we have one of the few instances where a sloping roof was removed in favour of a flat one.

Most churches underwent restoration of one kind or another in Victorian times, destroying much of our medieval heritage. Petit doggedly and persistently opposed this from 1841, and eventually the conservationists won. Alrewas' flat roofs are a symbol of a partial victory.

But there is the second question of whether achieving symmetrical roofs improved or detracted from its character?

Petit once remarked 'Yet I fear that even a judicious restoration would destroy many characteristic features, which in a building that stands in a manner alone, are the more valuable.'

He also talks a lot of the wonderful harmony in asymmetry especially when graced with dignity of age. But it would be another century before that concept would become understood. Designers and builders have a natural propensity to do symmetry for good reason, and it takes especial skill to go beyond that. Taken to extremes one gets suburbs and estates where everything looks the same. But getting asymmetry right, without looking disjointed, is harder. In Alrewas, judging by the picture, they really accomplished it for a few centuries.

Do look inside if the church is open. If the outside is no longer as extraordinary, the inside certainly is, and full of character.

4.1. Iron Works, near Wolverhampton, 1852 or '53, 27 × 38. From the angle and distance to St Peter's in the background, and the size of the works, this is likely to be the Spring Vale works which later became Bilston. It is one of the earliest known pictures of the Black Country in full flow, albeit the picture itself is worse for neglect. The largest Petit family landholding was the Ettingshall Estate, not far from here.

Tour 4

From Wolverhampton: Truth and Style

This tour combines the unusual destination of Wolverhampton with some wonderful villages, especially Tong over the border in Shropshire.

The Black Country is not the top rated tourist destination in the UK, and its biggest city Wolverhampton is not on most visitors' travel plans. It does not help itself with the lists of attractions found on travel websites, which are off-putting. But here I encourage you to see it as it was and is. It is one of the few places in the book where the present is much better than the past.

Wolverhampton was not always unappreciated. In 1834 White's *Gazette of Staffordshire* claims that it was 'salubrious and picturesque', despite the mines and factories to the south and east, because on its hills the breeze quickly dispersed the dirt, and because of the wonderful views west to the rolling hills in the distance.

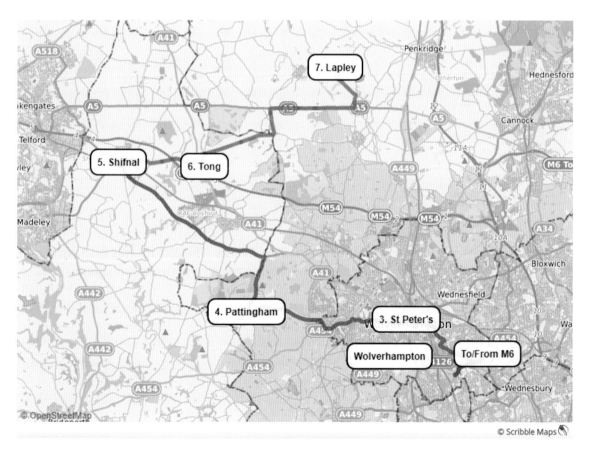

Its attractions then were helped by a much smaller population. By the mid-1830s the population had doubled over the beginning of the century from 24,000 to 48,000 – but that hardly compares with the 248,000 who now fill the modern town. Yet the pictures show that in the industrial areas it was indeed Dickensian.

Petit's pictures of Wolverhampton are some of the most interesting in this book, because the reality of those days was barely recorded. But I have to warn the reader that of the three stops in the city only St Peters will give that warm glow of a beautiful place visited and something new learnt. The first two places are educational but warm glows are only noticeable by their absence. Wolverhampton is still a gritty industrial city, albeit much pleasanter than before. In the first two stops we rummage around in the industrial areas and suburbs of the city, and then move on to St Peter's and the later village churches where interest and peaceful beauty again meet up. For a sanitized version of what the pictures in 4.1 and 4.2 show, there is the Black Country Museum at Dudley DY1 4SQ. We describe the route approaching from the M6, but of course there are many other ways to get to Bilston.

4.1 BILSTON, BLACK COUNTRY ROUTE, BILSTON, WV14 0UW

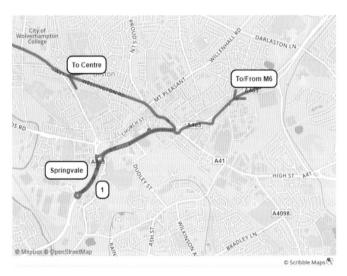

From junction 10 on the M6 follow the Black Country Route for three miles to the junction with the A41, then continue to the next roundabout before returning with a 360 U-turn back to the A41. If you wish, drive into the Springvale Retail Park.

You will have driven past what was the biggest, most profitable, steel works in England, which looked much like the picture here until well into the 1960s, now replaced with the giant warehouses of Britain's most successful retailers.

This was the location of the Springvale Iron Works, later to become Bilston Steel Works. The picture was made in 1853, I would guess from further away than along the road between the two roundabouts. Coseley Road, the postcode above, leads to an area called Highfields, but it is now just a neat suburb, with few views to be had. Back to the picture; notice the pit ponies to the left and the other chimneys in the background before what might be St Peter's church tower. The condition of the picture matches the subject; it was at the bottom of a pile and so more likely to rot. Not being picturesque, one imagines, to Petit's descendants, especially the smog and smoke from the chimneys, it is probably lucky to have survived. It is the earliest known accurate yet evocative picture of Victorian iron works.

Yet Petit's own ideas on what was picturesque were very different:

4.2a. Near Wolverhampton, c. 1835, 14 x 20. A very early picture of an unromantic subject. The Petits also owned the land under the Sedgeley Beacon, with good views, but not right for these pictures.

If picturesqueness is a merit, I can answer for it that the most picturesque objects I have seen are buildings of the most strictly utilitarian character, without a speck of ornament, and you may be sure erected at no more cost than was deemed necessary, without the slightest attention whatever to appearance. I speak of the furnaces in the neighbourhood of Wolverhampton. Some of these taken as buildings independently of their accompaniments of fire and smoke, are absolutely grand. There is something, too, very impressive, to my mind, in the lines of modern fortification…

Judging by this no-doubt deliberately provocative quote from one of his speeches (on Utilitarianism in Architecture) it is quite possible that this picture was exhibited to support this passage. One hundred years later we indeed started listing the grandest factories and power stations.
Take the A41 towards the centre.

4.2 Mines, wv1 3dz

These two pictures give, firstly, an impression of two mines as they were in the 1830s, and, secondly, the landscape around a smelting kiln. These images from the 1830s are just as rare as the one above. While there are one or two romanticised views of Dudley Castle, neither commercial artists nor amateurs would bother with something like this. It would be a further forty years until a later generation of artists attempted something comparable, and nearly a century before Lowry found a different way to capture similar themes in the factories around Manchester.

The postcode given is for the bridge over the canal at the end of Qualcast Road. To the east the view is towards an intensive mining area. Looking towards town, you cannot see the tower of

4.2b. Near Wolverhampton, 1830s, 15 × 21. A mystery, but again a rare picture of the Black Country around Wolverhampton in the 1830s.

St Peter's although it was clearly visible in Petit's day. The canal footpath can be reached through wasteland just the other (western) side of the bridge; but I cannot recommend it. Not dangerous, just litter-strewn and ugly. Walking along the bank of the canal itself is possible, a new asphalted track has been laid, presumably to attract cyclists, but the view is of the backs of industrial buildings.

The South Staffordshire coalfield was one of the richest in the country. It extended to the east of Wolverhampton, well within the city limits. The thick, easily accessible seams of coal were interlaced with iron ore, the base material for metal manufacturing. Wolverhampton became known internationally for the quality and variety of its metal parts. There was an intense concentration of shafts south of the A4124 Wednesfield Way, east of the canal, and north of Willenhall Road, the A454. In the first view there are churches in the distance, but I am not certain that it was taken from this area. An alternative suggestion is that the churches are those in Dudley to the south.

The second picture is a complete puzzle. There were many such kilns around Wolverhampton, alongside the remaining pasture land, and one cannot be certain if that is just a sludge puddle or if it is moving water. While we still pay a visible price for our creature comforts, on balance the Black Country looks far better now than it did then. Some of the character has been lost, but in this case perhaps that is no bad thing.

4.3 St Peter's Collegiate Church, Lichfield Street and Wulfruna Street, Wolverhampton. Parking at Civic Centre car park, WV1 1RQ

A magnificent church, with a remarkable group of pictures to accompany it.

Artistically these examples together illustrate how Petit's style evolved over the years: the dark, brooding mood of the early 1830s, the lighter gentler reconciliation in the early 1840s, and the terracotta sketches of the late 1840s and then 1853 when the major restoration was

4.3a. St Peter's, Wolverhampton, c. 1835, 29 × 24. Showing the nave and chancel before enlargement in the 1850s.

4.3b. St Peter's, c. 1840, 30 × 20, reproduction by permission of Wolverhampton Art Gallery. From the north side, still showing the cross on the tower.

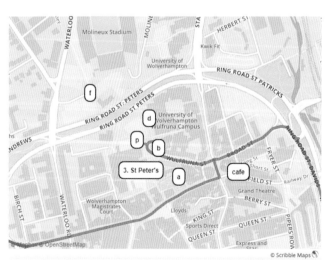

underway. The differences in part reflect his changing mood, and in part his changing attention and focus. Yet they are all beautiful depictions of the church that convey its ancient character.

The history of St Peter's Collegiate Church reaches back to the tenth century and the grant of ten hides of land at Hampton to the Lady Wulfrun (hence Wulfrun's Hampton abbreviated to Wolverhampton) by King Ethelred. The Church lands and the town were practically synonymous until the industrial revolution and the emergence of mining and metalwork based on the coal and iron nearby. St Peter's kept its independence from the Church of England until a special Act of 1848 that abolished the College and turned over the Church and subsidiary parishes to the Lichfield Diocese.

Petit captures the pride of its independence that lasted on or off for 900 years. The church looks and feels old, in the pictures. Compare with the present, how chancel and nave either side of the tower match with their correctly Gothic roofs. The wider nave diminishes the stature of the tower. Larger windows bring more light inside.

The nave and the chancel were rebuilt between 1852 and 1865 widening the interior. The St Peter's that we

4.3c. St Peter's, c. 1848, 36 × 25. From the south east. The cross is no longer on the tower.

4.3d. St Peter's, 1852 or 53, 27 × 37. A similar view to b, only from further back, and now restoration work has started. A pinnacle has been removed from the tower to accommodate the crane.

4.3e. Interior, St Peter's, 1830s, 25 × 21. The stone lion on the balustrade is not so well drawn, but then the sculpture does not look like a lion either.

see in the pictures and what is still visible inside is fifteenth-century. Has it been improved? Additional space was needed, but some of the changes seem unnecessary. Perhaps a tiny fraction of the dignity and power in the watercolours been eroded; or it may be the effect of the surrounding buildings that diminishes it a little.

The fourth picture was drawn from near the entrance to the car park in 1853 shortly after restoration had begun. One can see that the chancel has already come down, as has one of the tall pinnacles on the tower to avoid damage by the crane.

As ever, Petit does not seem to have painted it after its restoration and expansion. It is not a redevelopment that Petit is known to have commented on, and compared with many others, it seems to have retained much of the character of the old church – as much as might be allowed while the new town crowds it in.

Besides the exterior, the interior was and remains very impressive, as the fifth of this group shows. I was always puzzled by the mysterious creature to the right of the pulpit, thinking perhaps it was an artistic joke, but as ever I found Petit's takes practically no artistic licence. The lion on the balustrade is unique and worth the visit by itself. I cannot say that the picture, in this instance captures exactly the right effect as one sees it now, but the lion is indeed weird

4.3f. St Peter's, view, c. 1835, 24 × 31. From West Park, showing it was always an open space.

and can look like a ghostly presence from the north aisle. According to a kind member of the church, the story is that it was sculpted before anyone knew what a real lion looked like.

St Peters has the second oldest complete ring of 12 bells in the country. The bells are rung on Mondays for practice and at the Sunday service.

This last view is from the area that now includes West Hill Park. The correct angle, but a bit closer in, can be seen at the top of Whitmore Hill, alongside the archive building at WV1 1SF. This is accessible by taking the under-pass under the main road. If you visit West Hill Park it is possible to catch sight of St Peters but not at the correct angle, more round to the line of the nave. This seems to have been taken somewhere close to the schools between New Hampton Road E and Park Road East.

Finding pleasant refreshment in the centre of Wolverhampton is not so easy. There is a café in the town art gallery just on the east side of St Peter's. The gallery is well worth a visit while you are here; and 100 yards round the corner in Lichfield Street is an Indian café Zuri – an unusual and pleasant experience by comparison with the routine chains that one finds everywhere.

4.4 Pattingham, St Chad's Church, Patshull Road, Staffordshire, WV6 7BQ

Seven miles and about twenty-five minutes west of the centre of Wolverhampton, after a drive through its wealthier and more attractive suburbs.

Petit's picture dates from about 1843. The church, which in the main dates from the early thirteenth century, was substantially rebuilt after Petit painted it, culminating with the addition of a spire in 1871. If it were just the spire, this might be an improvement that I would not judge too harshly. It is clearly an addition, yet adds grandeur and seems proportionate.

4.4. Pattingham, c. 1843, 20 × 25. Showing the chancel and tower before 'improvements'.

4.4b. Pattingham. Illustration in *Remarks on Architectural Character* no. XXII (22).

Petit was particularly taken with the chancel of Pattingham church (noting the hoods above the windows) and this picture is illustrated in *Remarks on Architectural Character* (1845). An unattributed copy of the illustration hangs on the north west pillar inside the church. In searching for forms and proportions which give churches that special character of being dignified, conducive to spiritual feeling, and above all beautiful to the eye, one can see something special in the chancel, which the watercolour captures. However, this is hard to appreciate in the current scene where the nave has been pushed up and the roofs harmonised. So, besides the spire, I find that the other changes diminished the character.

The pub opposite serves food all day and has a nice view of the church.

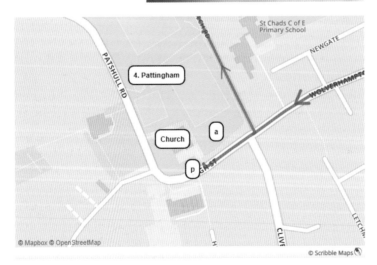

4.5a. St Andrew's, Shifnal, c. 1839, 22 × 25. From the south west. At this time Petit lived in Shifnal, and this was his local church.

4.5 St Andrew's Church, Church Street, Shifnal, Shropshire tf11 9ab

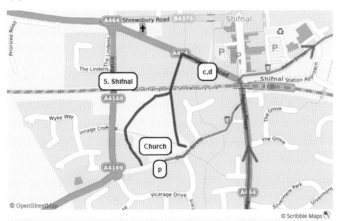

Next we journey some nine miles further west over the county border to Shifnal, but still in the diocese of Lichfield and the old kingdom of Mercia.

Petit resigned from active parish work in 1834 to concentrate on his writing and painting; he lived in Shifnal for twelve years while writing his first books until subsequently moving to the family home in Lichfield. He

4.5b. St Andrew's, Shifnal, c. 1842, 25 × 18, the Ian Cooke Collection. From the north side.

4.5c. Interior St Andrew's, c. 1842, 28 × 24, the Ian Cooke Collection.

painted Shifnal church from just about every angle, although he never used its exterior (except for the windows) in his writing, presumably because, despite good features, he never thought it one of the very best.

Here are five pictures, the last four of which are all from one album made in 1842, while the first is probably from just a year or two earlier. The first two are of the church from different sides. The angle of the first you will find at the corner of the churchyard and Church Street, although the correct distance is not possible to find because of the wall and buildings on the other side of the road. The second picture is on the other side, and the third an interior to compensate if the church is locked.

The fourth and fifth pictures need some little effort. They appear to be taken from the bridge over the stream on Victoria Road (c, d on the map), just past the Jasper Arms pub. This can be accessed by the lane, Church Walk, to the north of the churchyard on the other side from Church Street. The fifth picture is from the same bridge but looking the other way. Now, unfortunately this is not the most beautiful part of Shifnal.

St Andrew's dates from the twelfth century, but underwent extensive renovation in the 1870s after these pictures by Petit. Compare the pictures with the present structure, which still dominates the town, but not to the same extent, or with the same character. Petit admired its windows for their

4.5d. Shifnal Church View, c. 1842, 25 × 20, the Ian Cooke Collection. From the river bridge.

4.5e. In Shifnal, c. 1842, 25 × 20, the Ian Cooke Collection. Looking in the opposite direction to d.

varied tracery – i.e. the design of the structural parts of the window, not the glass. He presented some of them in *Remarks on Architectural Character*. They showed both variety and harmony. If you walk around the church you will notice the interesting old windows by comparison with the later, more boring ones. This is a taster for even better windows in tour 5.

4.6 St Bartholomew's Church, Tong, Shropshire, tf11 8pw

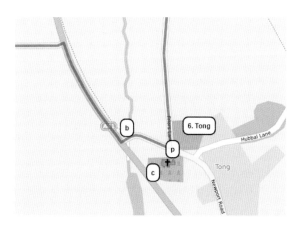

From Shifnal, we turn back east and it is only just over three miles and less than ten minutes to the un-missable object of the detour into Shropshire. For Petit, and for us today, Tong is one of the jewels in the diocese of Lichfield, and indeed in the country – original and largely unspoilt. It is one of few churches that was not diminished by the craze for Gothic restoration which Petit fought against. Unfortunately, though, its stature has been significantly damaged since by the proximity of the A41.

4.6a. St Bartholomew's, Tong, c. 1842, 25 × 20, the Ian Cooke Collection. This is the view that Petit reproduced for his article on Tong in the *Archaeological Journal*.

Petit wrote an article for the second volume of the *Archaeological Journal* (1845) solely devoted to extolling Tong. The first picture is the view included in the article mentioned. The second is a view over the pond, the remnants of which are down the road just before the junction with the A41. In dry weather one can get round to the same spot.

The Archaeological Institute, together with its journal, had been founded the year before to provide a forum through which preservation-minded gentlemen might counter the increasingly strident calls for everything to be built or rebuilt copying middle Gothic. Tong provided a wonderful example of a fifteenth-century church and Petit points out how, for example, its flattened roofs and broad tower, as well as the lack of perfect symmetry all contribute to the wonderful harmony of the building.

Specifically about the tower he wrote: 'if we compare this central octagon and spire with any in Germany, where this feature is a common one, though it is exceedingly rare in England, we shall have no reason to pronounce that our own specimen suffers by comparison.'

4.6b. St Bartholomew's, Tong, c. 1843, 21 × 25. From the pond, showing the lights on inside the church at dusk.

4.6c. St Bartholomew's, Tong, c. 1843, 25 × 34, showing flooding, from the north.

4.6e. Interior, St Bartholomew's, Tong, c. 1842, 24 × 20, the Ian Cooke Collection.

4.6d. St Bartholomew's, Tong, c. 1842, 24 × 20, the Ian Cooke Collection. From the churchyard.

He ends by saying:

I fear I shall be thought by some to have intruded too much of mere opinion and criticism of matters of taste, into a journal devoted to antiquarian research, but I would plead in my defence that it is within the province of archaeology not merely to establish dates or certify historical facts but also to encourage a true appreciation of the relics bequeathed to us as indications of the spirit, character and genius of a former age.

This was not meant to be a platitude – but a wake-up call to his colleagues that archaeology and research is fine, but it needs to be used to save the relics from destruction. Elsewhere (in an article on Gloucestershire) he says:

many precious objects have been irreparably lost… by the zeal of persons who consider the neat and perfect appearance of new work to be more suitable to a church, than the dignity resulting from the gradual impression of ages, and the force of long associations.

The third picture is from the opposite corner, practically in the road, and seems to have been made when the local stream had flooded. The church is beautiful from literally every angle and I especially recommend the far left corner as you enter the gate, which is where the fourth is from.

4.6f. The Tong Cup, c. 1842, 24 × 18, the Ian Cooke Collection. The cup has since been moved to Lichfield for safe-keeping.

Tong also featured in both Petit's first two books and so is one of very few buildings that he discusses three times. It is, of course, listed in guide books, and features in Simon Jenkins's *England's Thousand Best Churches*, but I (and I think Petit) would say it is much better and more important than one among a thousand. It offers one of the best examples of harmonious architecture anywhere to be found, beautiful yet awe-inspiring, as befits any place of worship, both in the details and the whole.

I include a picture of the interior, which may be locked, and one of the celebrated Tong Cup which has since been removed to Lichfield Cathedral.

From here we take you back to Staffordshire and to an unusual church and landscape.

4.7 All Saints Church, Lapley, Staffordshire, ST19 9JS

From Tong we continue roughly north east, for fifteen minutes and nine miles to the village of Lapley, much of the journey on dead-straight Roman roads, the A5 (Watling Street) and then a north-western route to Chester. A mile further along the A5 there was an important Roman way-station and fortified town, Pennocrucium, which was identified from the air in 1946. It sat astride routes to Wroxeter, Chester, Lichfield and the south.

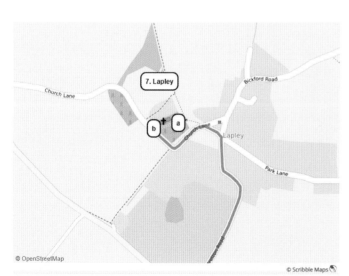

Lapley was and is a small village where there was once a small Benedictine Priory, now the parish church. The first picture is a landscape view west. At first I thought that it must be from the top of the tower, because the countryside is flat hereabouts, and so I arranged to get access, thanks to the great kindness of the Vicar and warden, but not so. The church sits on a slight rise and the view is that seen from the entrance, but looking more north than directly opposite the

4.7a. Lapley, 1830s, 12 × 26. Looking west towards Wheaton Aston. A windmill is visible in the distance, but not the church, which was yet to be built.

4.7b. Lapley, c. 1842, 24 × 20, the Ian Cooke Collection. From the churchyard, with scaffolding around the tower.

church. Since the trees near the wall are likely to have been there in Petit's day, he might have sat just between the tree and wall. Notice the blob in the middle of the picture. Apparently this is the old windmill that once stood in Mill Lane at Wheaton Aston. The church at Wheaton Aston had not yet been built.

The second view is from the other side of the graveyard looking back to the east window of the church. Today the tower buttresses are bigger than they appear in the picture and one might wonder if the scaffolding shown in the picture had something to do with the need to improve the tower's support.

Tour 5

Central Staffordshire: Windows, Ruins and Estates

This tour starts on the outskirts of Stafford, taking in three interesting but relatively obscure spots before tackling a couple of serious but rarely visited churches, Staffordshire's best ruined abbey, and two remarkable old estates, at Alton and nearby Wootton. If you need to shorten the route do 5.1 to 5.3 separately from 5.4 to 5.8.

This tour might be better done outside school holidays if you contemplate the stop at Alton. Indeed probably better to do it between November and the end of March. Otherwise one risks getting caught up in the nightmare of Alton Towers traffic. Unless of course that is your primary destination.

However we start with a bridge. Not many bridges feature in tours, which is a shame, because they are important architectural features too; fortunately this one happens to be en route. Of course the biggest bridges are rightly famous and get considerable design attention, here we see the smallest of the three we visit in Staffordshire.

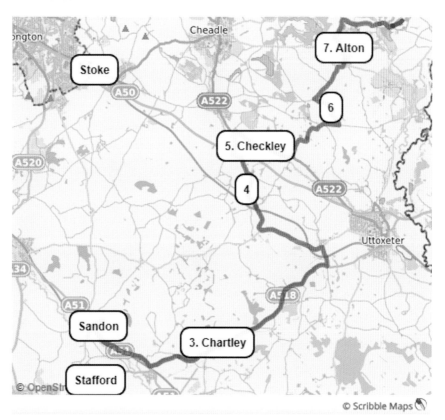

5.1. Sandon Bridge, 1820s, 8 × 12. The old bridge over the river Trent. The painting appears to be one of the earliest, judging by its size and the mount.

5.1 SANDON BRIDGE, SANDON, ST18 0DH

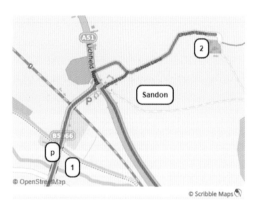

Sandon Bridge is four miles north east of Stafford along the B5066, Sandon Road. Petit's view shows a famous old crossing point of the river Trent. The road crosses the river and 100 yards beyond the Trent and Mersey canal, where one can park and access the canal path eastwards. One can then cross the field to the riverbank and see the very utilitarian modern bridge, unlike the old one, or indeed the old canal bridge. Definitely not an improvement from an architectural point of view, I think.

5.2 CHURCH OF ALL SAINTS, CHURCH LANE, SANDON, STAFFORD, ST18 0DB

From here it is a short hop to the remarkably positioned Sandon Church. The picture is small and early – from the 1820s at a guess – and not in good condition. In 1831 there were 558 inhabitants of the parish of Sandon, similar to now.

In the eighteenth century the first Baron Harrowby bought the estate and, in the process of creating a park around the new Sandon Hall that he planned, had the whole village moved away from the church. This incongruity has remained ever since and the church stands somewhat isolated.

The church was extensively remodelled in 1851, to serve as a private chapel for the Earls of Harrowby and it was restored again in 1923. In the churchyard there is the extraordinary tomb of the former owner of the then more modest manor, and the last of his family, Sampson Erdeswick,

5.2. Sandon Church, 1820s, 11 × 21. Also a very early picture, before Petit developed a distinctive style.

who is reported to have lost his mind before fashioning this tomb two years before he died in 1603. Despite its roughness the picture seems important because it is possibly the only one that shows the appearance of the old village church before the remodelling, at least to the extent that the trees in the picture do not block the view. It was clearly taken from the north-west side, about where the road is, but maybe it is best compared from closer, within the churchyard. The differences to the nave and chancel are hard to determine, but the tower is very different. I find the present pinnacles rather incongruous compared with the characterful and more harmonious old tower in the picture.

Still the position is unbeatable.

5.3 CHARTLEY CASTLE, ST18 0LN – DRIVE BY

Continue to join the A51, Chartley Castle is only five miles away, along the A518. It is a remarkable sight from the road, but that, unfortunately is all one can see. It stands on private property, and is only open to the public on a couple of days each year.

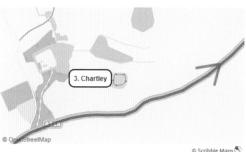

In Petit's day the road may have been closer to the castle, and the place where he sat to paint can be guessed, allowing for the fact that the walls have crumbled and the ground accumulated since his time here.

Despite the degradations of the structure, Chartley is still one of the most interesting ruins in Staffordshire and worth a drive-by, even if only to take in the view of it.

5.3. Chartley Castle, 1830s, 16 × 28. The ruin has crumbled further and is rarely accessible.

The castle was abandoned as a residence in 1485 after the Battle of Bosworth, the new lord taking up residence in Chartley Manor, a mile down the road, where Mary, Queen of Scots, was held for a while. Petit captures the feeling of medieval history in his picture, before the Tudor shenanigans.

Now to a couple of churches, simple ones, rarely visited.

5.4 ALL SAINTS, CHURCH LEIGH, STOKE-ON-TRENT, ST10 4RD

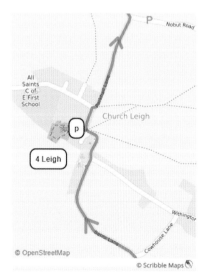

Church Leigh is eight miles and 15 minutes away east and then north. Petit visited Leigh on several occasions because he was struck by the simple beauty of the church. He painted it from every angle, inside and out, mostly around 1837/8 but also earlier.

The first picture is the one that he copied into *Remarks*, commenting:

> As a complete cross church, with side aisles to the nave, I will point out Leigh Staffordshire. The central tower is perfectly plain … its extreme simplicity and admirable proportion give it a grandeur which has often failed to strike me in much richer buildings; but it is very clear such a tower could have stood nowhere but at the intersection

5.4a. All Saints, Church Leigh, c. 1839, 23 × 30. From the north west. The view that Petit eventually uses in *Remarks*, vol. 2, p. 44.

5.4b. All Saints, Church Leigh, c. 1838, 23 × 30. From the west. As Petit says, the church 'Should be visited by the architect and the antiquary…it exhibits a very peculiar description of decorated'.

5.4c. All Saints, Church Leigh, c. 1839, 27 × 22. From the east, with a different roof and '…square-headed windows with very bold tracery', which has since been replaced.

5.4d. All Saints, Church Leigh, c. 1838, 25 x 23. Showing some of the remarkable tracery, which complements the simplicity of the tower.

of the cross … The inside is interesting although defaced by plaster ceilings: it contains a curious font, of early English, if not Norman character.

Given that Petit was drawing on examples from all over the UK, France, and bits of the rest of Europe, it is significant. It still has a lovely feel. Interestingly the church was renovated in 1846, including the tower, but fortunately its important architectural features remained unchanged.

The different coloured roof, shown in picture 3, adds to the harmony, but sadly this was altered, slightly weakening the impression.

Now is the moment to delve a little into Gothic windows. This also was a matter of great debate, including whether stained glass narratives could continue across tracery or whether each piece of glass should stand alone. Remarkably, Petit finds three churches all close by to illustrate beautiful window tracery: here, and at our next stop, Checkley, and in Norbury (see 6.5)

In particular, if you walk around Leigh you will see that the tracery of the windows is exceptionally varied. This ensures that the simple church does not become dull. William Morris and Sir Edward Burne-Jones added to the west window here – a rare example of an obvious improvement.

The church is usually locked so you would need to telephone in advance to see inside.

5.4e. Interior, All Saints, Church Leigh, c. 1838, 27 × 22. Petit comments 'the nave is detached from the chancel by the (supports) for the tower…central arches highly pointed'. This picture shows the interior before renovation.

5.4f. Font, All Saints, Church Leigh, c. 1838, 13 × 17. 'A curious font of early English, if not Norman, character'.

5.5 St Mary's, Checkley, Stoke-on-Trent, st10 4nj

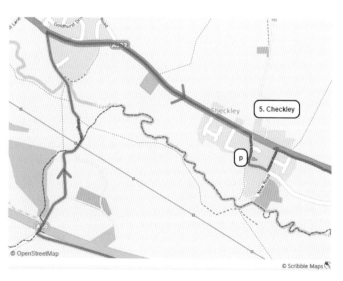

The next church is just a few miles distant on the other side of the A50, five minutes away. Again you are likely to be the only visitor.

The key aspect that clearly attracted Petit was the East End, the window and the crenellated (ie small battlements) roof. Fortunately you can access the exact spot, even if the church itself is locked. The thing to notice, besides its dramatic shape are the little roses at the intersections of the stone above the five lancets of the window. A late thirteenth-century decoration that is

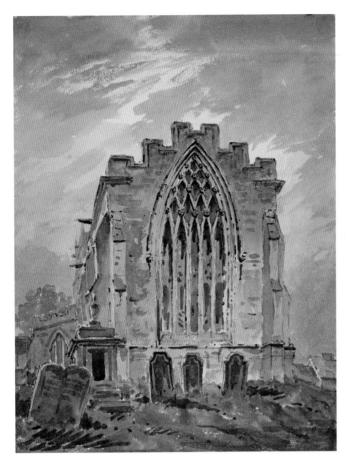

5.5a. St Mary's, Checkley, c. 1838, 36 × 26. The remarkable east end.

5.5b. Interior, St Mary's, Checkley, c. 1838, 27 × 21. The same window from inside.

very rare and special – 'fleuron decorations at the intersections of the tracery' – is the proper name, since you ask. Petit found it, and now you have too. Without Petit, I, at least, would never have understood how this particular detail can make the whole a little more beautiful.

Norbury (6.4) has some roses too, but if you want a rose-mullioned selfie, these are the best. It seems more than a coincidence that there are three beautifully adorned windows at churches so close to each other in this off-the-beaten-track corner of Staffordshire–Derbyshire. Petit speculated that they were all done by a local long-forgotten craftsman. You will see in the image that all three were selected for inclusion in his illustration of windows in *Remarks*. As is shown by the

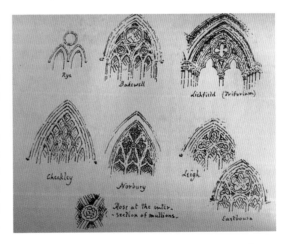

5.5c Examples of tracery, p. 175, vol. 2, *Remarks on Church Architecture*.

96

5.6a. Croxden Abbey, c. 1839, 23 × 19. There is much left of the abbey today, but these pictures are still hard to pin down precisely.

picture of the interior, the window looks good from the inside as well, although again a phone call in advance is needed to see it.

Petit's first book grappled with exactly what makes beauty in architecture, and church architecture in particular, because of its centrality in life for most people at the time. He was the first to try to do this on a massive scale, visiting and drawing many hundreds of churches and then selecting three hundred to illustrate his points. For many his book was the height of excellence in architectural appreciation at the time, but for a vociferous few it was anathema. Beauty for them had no place in matters of religion; churches had to be built or rebuilt according to rules – divinely inspired rules which Pugin, Ruskin, and the dogmatists of the Ecclesiological Society felt that only they could perceive accurately.

Fortunately Checkley and Leigh churches more or less fell within those rules so they survived the Gothic revival intact. But the question of beauty in architecture and how to achieve it has certainly not gone away. As Petit sought to explain, it is important, once a building has fulfilled its function. Any historical (or modern) style can be beautiful, if it is well executed. Hence his view that form and proportions are critical, not rules about a style.

Now for something more comfortably relaxing.

5.6b. Croxden Abbey, 1830s, 24 × 15.

5.6 CROXDEN ABBEY, CROXDEN, ST14 5JF

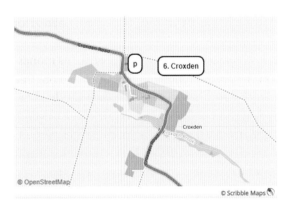

Less than five miles and ten minutes north west from here along back roads is the remarkable ruin of Croxden Abbey; perhaps the best ancient abbey in Staffordshire. It has changed a little since Petit's day. It is not that easy to see where each of the pictures was made, and I will not spoil the fun. These are four of at least six known pictures that Petit drew, one of which is dated April 1838. Judging by the style, I think the others were either then or within a few years of that date.

5.6c. Croxden Abbey, c. 1839, 31 x 23.

5.6d. Croxden Abbey, 1838, 27 × 18. A precise date given on the mount. a and c are probably a year later when Petit was writing the subject in pencil top left.

Abbeys and monasteries were major institutions in the Middle Ages up until the reformation in the sixteenth century. They were by and large self-supporting, running farms and educational centres – the good side – sometimes corrupt and predatory on the neighbouring population – the bad side. While some had earlier origins, by the time of their Dissolution by Henry VIII, most had been built or re-built by Norman nobles for the benefit of their and their family's souls, often penance for misdeeds including murder, torture, misappropriation and more.

That brings us to Petit's objection to the Gothic Revivalists. Imagine Croxden when all its monastic buildings were standing (there is a drawing given on the board at the site). As he pointed out that is Gothic, real Gothic. A product of the cruelty, greed and devil-take-the-hindmost attitude of the age (there were hugely bloody civil wars every century during the Gothic era between the eleventh and fifteenth centuries). Wonderful buildings, finding their purest expression in cathedrals, abbeys and monasteries, but savage.

For Petit and others Victorian Gothic was (and perhaps remains) copy Gothic, and thus a bit twee. In his view 'the highest praise is that a thing may be taken for something it is not.' In contrast,

5.7a. Alton Bridge, 1820s or 30s, 19 × 13. An early picture, not so well preserved.

he urged: 'The builder…will thus learn, not to imitate, but to invent, perhaps to mark the period of his labours by a style distinguished from that of his ancestors otherwise than by its meagerness and deformity.'

And that is what Petit tried to do in the two buildings he designed himself: his summer house, Bumblekyte (see Figs. 1.7a and b) and St Philips, Caerdeon, near Barmouth, North Wales (Fig. 9.13, p. 169 shows this remarkable – non-gothic, Victorian – church).

Visiting Croxden is important not just for what it is, but for the understanding it gives about the Gothic revival and all the destruction and dull conformity it led to, as well as a few good Victorian-Gothic buildings by the best proponents.

And so on to two aristocratic estates.

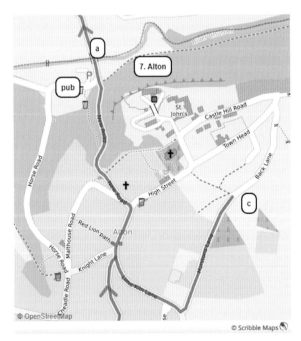

5.7 ALTON, FARLEY LANE, ST10 4BY

Alton is only three miles north of Croxden. Most visitors who flock to Alton today are going to the theme park. However, for those for whom this would be unthinkable, it is best to choose a moment when the park is closed. Alton, and its surroundings, as these pictures show, was always beautiful in and of itself.

The site of the first picture is the bridge as it looked then on Farley Lane at the post code given above, facing away from the Park, looking up towards the Castle. The hill above, shown closer in Fig. 5.7b, was the site of the old Alton Castle, of

5.7c. Alton, 1839. 12 × 21. A view back towards the ruin; it appears to have been drawn at sunset.

5.7b. Alton, 1839, 19 × 26. Showing the ruins before the castle was built, and a much more advanced picture than Fig. 5.7a.

which the few then-remaining ruins can be seen in all three pictures. There is a nice inn just below the bridge, quiet when the theme park is quiet.

Fig. 5.7c is a most interesting view towards the old ruined castle from the other side of Alton. You can get some impression of this at the beginning of Back Lane (see map), at the start of a footpath, where you can also see some of the new castle. Look the other way and there is the sense of rolling hills. The picture was probably drawn a bit further away along the footpath on the opposite side of the road, but absent many buildings around. At sunset, at least in Spring, the light can appear identical to how Petit captured it.

The three pictures date from the 1830s, just before Pugin began his sequence of major works for the sixteenth Earl of Shrewsbury, which would last until Pugin's death in 1852, including building the new castle. It is almost certainly no coincidence that Petit came to capture the ruins on the hill from all angles before they disappeared.

Petit regarded Pugin as the inspiration of the Gothic Revival movement and opposed not so much his work as his evangelical zeal and insistence that Gothic was 'self-evidently' the only correct style for churches. In a letter Petit recorded his belief that Pugin would in the future be seen to have been the best of those who tried to develop something *original* based on the Gothic style. This is indeed what we have seen at the end of tour 2 with Pugin's best church, not far from here at Cheadle. This is not at all the same thing as following the rules that others such as the Ecclesiologists were laying down.

As we have seen in chapter 1, the title and Alton estate of the Earl of Shrewsbury passed to the Chetwynd family of Ingestre when the old Earl died without heir. The subsequent ruin of the Alton estate dates from a breakdown in the relationship between the new Earl and his wife in 1896. Apparently the Earl refused to pay for upkeep of the palace in which his wife lived. Eventually it was auctioned off and the new owners asset stripped what they could sell, including even plaster off the walls, before it eventually found its way to the current owners.

Now, as at Trentham, private for-profit ownership has given Alton a new lease of life as a theme park. No-one I know who has visited the theme park notices the history, the buildings or the beauty of the environment in which it sits, just whether the rides are good. So for me Trentham does better in terms of preserving some sense of the origin of the estate. Most visitors to Alton Towers just find its beautiful location a nuisance to get to.

From here it is a very short step to Wootton (in Petit's day with one 't') Lodge, five minutes without traffic, which makes an interesting contrast to both the Trentham and Alton estates. The map points the route round by the theme park, the alternative to the south is about the same if that is what your satnav chooses.

5.8 Wootton Lodge, Waste Lane, Ashbourne, DE6 2GU

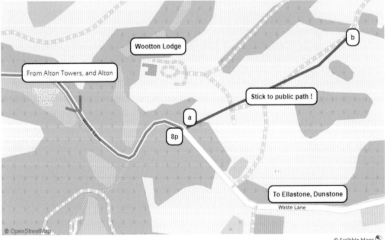

15–20 minute moderately steep but easy walk.

Depending on your satellite navigation, or map reading, you might enter Waste Lane from either direction. If you arrive from the east, you will pass the main entrance to Wootton Lodge and need to follow the road around the edge of the estate. Half a mile on is a side entrance on the right, twenty yards past

5.8a. Wootton Lodge, 1820s, 8 × 13. A small early picture drawn from a footpath through the estate.

5.8b. Wootton Lodge, c. 1838, 32 × 23. Petit is clearly more interested in capturing the tree and the land-scape than the house itself.

5.8c Near Wootton, 1838, 27 × 19. Looking towards the Weaver hills, the exact location not yet discovered.

which there is the first footpath through a gap in the wall behind a tree. The second footpath, the best for us, is a couple of hundred yards further down the road, through another gap in the wall, not behind a tree. There is a footpath sign on the opposite side of the road. You can park on the verge if not too muddy.

Arriving from the west, you come to the footpath just around a sharp right bend pointing up a quite steep hill.

While the views of the lodge at the key points are best in winter, the grounds are much more beautiful in the other seasons. So visits at all times of the year have their advantages.

I mention in the introduction about how many of the wealthy estates in Staffordshire were broken up, and we have now seen examples at Ingestre, Tixall, Hamstall Ridware, Trentham and just previously at Alton. The estate at Wootton Lodge is the exception. However, whereas the remains of the others are visible to the public, Wootton is very private.

In Petit's day the Lodge and surrounding land was owned by the Davenport family. Half a century ago it was bought by the Bamford family of JCB fame, who have extensively developed and preserved the original Grade I building; they use part of the park across the river as a JCB testing area.

There are however two little-publicized public footpaths onto the estate, which is all we need. The one we use is very worthwhile for a short visit to see how the Lodge looks by comparison to the old pictures. As you can see from the pictures Petit was interested in the Lodge in its natural setting, more than the Lodge itself.

As soon as you step through the wall and enter the grounds you glimpse the side view of the lodge (vegetation still permitting). This is the angle of the first picture, however its location might be further up the hill either on the road or on the other footpath where the view is blocked. Continue up the path, and you get a wonderful view of the extraordinary Elizabethan Lodge and its setting. If it reminds you a bit of Tixall Gatehouse that is not surprising as it was built just a few decades after, with the exterior steps added a hundred years later.

One can see how carefully the estate is being preserved, with new buildings above the path, all at considerable expense. After the intersection of footpaths, gradually the carefully chosen view of the second picture comes into focus. Continue on the lower path until you come to a broken tree. This is where I think the second picture was drawn from.

Compare this estate with the ruins at Trentham or the circus at Alton. Beautifully preserved, but only visible by squeezing through gaps in the wall and being subject to warnings to beware trespassing. And only visible thanks to our unique tradition of sacrosanct public footpaths. Long may they survive.

Note that Petit himself drew his pictures from the same paths. I had thought the positions would be impossible to find, but no. He also stuck to the paths and found the great views.

Both pictures shows the Weaver Hills in the background.

Mystery Picture, Near Wootton

The final picture in this tour should not be so much of a mystery, but I have not yet found this rocky outcrop, thinking it might be inside the grounds of the Lodge. It is titled 'Near Wootton' and presumably also shows part of the Weaver Hills in the distance. They will become more familiar in tour 6, which ends nearby in the village of Wootton.

6.1a. St Oswald's, Ashbourne, c. 1837, 33 × 23. This and the following two pictures show different aspects of the church, another which Petit painted from every angle in the late 1830s.

Tour 6

The Dove Valley: Six Weeks in 1838

While each tour has its distinctive attractions, this one is special because it is concentrated in a very small area – it could practically be done on foot – and because the pictures are similarly all from one period in the late 1830s. Indeed most are from March to May 1838. Petit chose this small region, around Ashbourne, Mayfield, Norbury and Ellastone, to spend about six weeks sketching in 1838 in preparation for his first book. At no other time in his life did he produce so many pictures in one small area.

I give quite a lot of pictures, and of course you can just do the ones that you want. There are a few places where walking is recommended, although a lot to see by car.

There is a reason to do this tour on a Friday or Saturday between April and October, because Norbury Manor, adjacent to the church, is open to the public for a few hours on those days, if that might be of interest.

While three of the four churches in the region: Ashbourne, Mayfield, and Norbury received a lot of attention from Petit, this trip is remarkable for the number of pure landscapes, or distant views

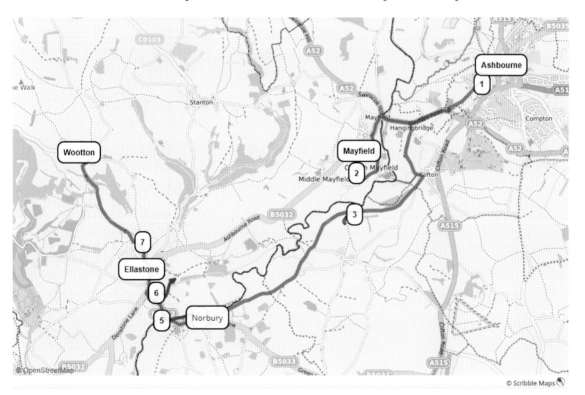

6.1b. St Oswald's, Ashbourne, c. 1837, 25 × 21. While the pictures show a deep appreciation of the church, yet it was not in the end included in his book.

of the churches, one after another, in which he seems to be experimenting with the style he would take onto the continent for his last preparatory trips for the first book, which came out in 1841. It was not the first time in this region, because a couple of the pictures are clearly from two different earlier periods, but at no later time in his career (that we know of) did he devote so much energy to landscape and sky, as opposed to buildings.

Apologies to purists who might resent a number of cross-border pictures intruding in a Staffordshire guide. Norbury and Ashbourne are but a step across the river Dove and Petit crossed and re-crossed it many times between March and May 1838.

We start in Ashbourne itself, although the tour is practically a circle and you could start at any other point.

6.1c. St Oswald's, Ashbourne, c. 1837, 25 × 23.

6.1d. Interior, St Oswald's, Ashbourne, c. 1837, 33 × 23. The reflected sunlight in this picture is remarkable.

6.1 St Oswald's Church, Ashbourne, 5 School Lane, Ashbourne, de6 1an

Parking is usually available on the street above the church. Ashbourne Church is remarkable in itself, and because, while Petit completed numerous watercolours of it, in the end it does not feature in any of his writings. By visiting it I think one can see why.

The first three pictures show a beautiful church in a rural setting. Unfortunately now we can only see the setting in the pictures; it is no longer rural, although the town is very pleasant anyway. Walking around the church within its grounds will enable you to see the first three angles from which he painted it. However the best view is to be found from the field above the church. Cross the road and to the left of the school is a footpath entrance to the field, from where you need to walk up to the hedge at the top. The hedge blocks the view from the road on the other side. While it is a remarkable church (others consider it the 'best' in Derbyshire), yet, apart from the spire, there is something less satisfactory about the rest of its architecture and that hesitation continues inside.

Perhaps I am imagining it. Petit, gentleman that he was, generally refrained from unnecessary criticism of churches, commenting once how they are the product of many different constraints at different times, and all have such important associations to those who care for them, so even when absolutely necessary, changes should be done very carefully. Ashbourne clearly did not serve his purposes for an illustration in one of his books, although he painted it from every possible angle.

6.1e. View of St Oswald's, Ashbourne, 1838, 26 × 18. Only this view of St Oswald's belongs to the same album as the more vibrant pictures of section 6.3.

Was it the bulk of the structure beneath the spire? Or a want of harmony among the different parts?

The exterior was hardly touched during the 1870s restoration by Gilbert Scott, by which time he had moved to a more preservationist stance. The crenellation (battlement) on the chancel roof he added and this seems to be no bad thing at all. Yet it is the spire that makes the church and, from a distance, it was clearly a wonderful sight; it is a shame that it is harder to find such views now.

The church is often open, and it is worth entering to see for yourself how well the architecture works, especially the double size north transept opposite the entrance. On the right, east, side of this are tombs of famous Ashbournians of the fourteenth and fifteenth centuries. The interior picture is attractive because of the light shown coming through the windows, although it depicts a rather untidy scene within.

The last picture is I think the approach from the north-west perhaps from the top of the market square, but there is no view there, nor from further up the street from the new church. But the town is pleasant to walk in and the best place on this tour for coffee and tea, although not for meals.

6.2a. St John the Baptist's, Church Mayfield, 1830s, 17 × 18. An unusual, more conventional early watercolour, where the scene is set with people.

6.2 CHURCH LANE, CHURCH MAYFIELD, MAYFIELD, ASHBOURNE, DE6 2JH

A short journey takes one to the neighbouring town/village of Mayfield. Of the three different neighbouring Mayfield villages, we want Church Mayfield.

The church is beautiful, though not perhaps as remarkable as Norbury or Ashbourne. Unlike Ashbourne it is rarely visited and you will probably be able to enjoy it and the surrounding setting, which is still very attractive, by yourself. This picture of it seems significantly earlier than 1838 and focuses on the picturesque village setting, rather than the architecture. Other pictures are very likely to have been made on the 1838 trip, when the interior, the second picture, was also painted, but the exteriors from that trip have not yet been located.

6.2b. Interior, St John the Baptist's, Church Mayfield, 1838, 29 × 22.

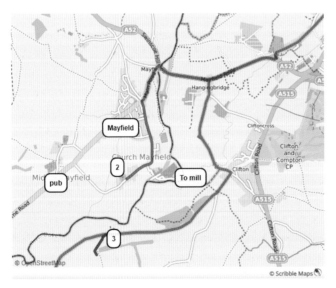

The picture appears to have been taken from Church Lane, just before one reaches the church if you are coming from the Ashbourne direction. Notice the old barn building standing end-on beside the road. It is the same as that in the picture. However, it seems to have been considerably raised in height since Petit's day, as shown by the walls. Further away, on the other side of the road is a black telephone pole against the wall of a house's front garden. This is where the picture was painted. Was the barn so low that so much of the church tower would have been visible? One does not know.

6.8c. Factory near Ashbourne, 1830s, 19 x 17. By the river Dove, still in existence.

Either way, the picture is much closer to the typical picturesque village scenes of professional artists, and unlike Petit's rougher, more impressionistic style that we see most of the time, and that he had reached by the mid-1830s. Notice how the person contributes to this cosy rustic feel. Again typical of conventional artists of the day who artfully dressed and placed people and domestic animals to evoke the atmosphere of the scene – artifice that Petit later avoided entirely. It shows that he could do such work if he wanted, and that most of the time he did not choose to, preferring to capture more objectively the effect of the church, its setting or the scenery itself. On the one hand it is a beautiful picture, but on the other hand not so uniquely Petit.

From the other side of the church you can see up to the high ground of 6.3, and there is an informative plaque near the churchyard gate on that side.

The 1834 *Gazetteer* mentions two cotton mills one near Mayfield and one just across the river in Derbyshire, one of which is shown in the next picture. It is very likely that these were situated where the current factory is between two branches of the river, accessed by the road which you will have passed just before reaching the church. While there is one other factory site a little further upstream, it does not straddle the Dove and may not be old as this is.

6.3a. Ashbourne and Mayfield, 1838, 14 × 23. This shows the spire of Ashbourne glinting in the sun, in contrast to Fig. 6.3b.

There is a footpath from the other side although I have not taken it since this picture was discovered. The Rose and Crown in Middle Mayfield back on the main road is an exceptionally good pub for food. The Dunscombe Arms, further on in Ellastone where we will end, is one of the best restaurants in Staffordshire. But now we return back initially towards Ashbourne. Turn right across the river, passing the footpath towards the factory and turn right in the village of Clifton to get to the road, Sides Lane, alongside the Dove on the other side of the river.

6.3 Views of Ashbourne and Mayfield, de6 2en

This stop involves a twenty-minute round-trip walk, quite steep, but worth it, especially if the conditions are a bit sunny.

Along Sides Lane, there is a footpath sign to the left just after one to the right. The footpath points off into the field on the right, up a fairly steep hill. You will need to tuck a car onto the verge, possibly on the other side, as tightly as possible, shown as point P on map.

Walk up to the tree line diagonally right to point a. We are seeking the location of a remarkable series of views showing the churches of Ashbourne and Mayfield in the distance. There are several

6.3b. Ashbourne and Mayfield, 1838, 13 × 18. This shows how the spire of Ashbourne can be difficult to make out without the reflection of the sun. Both pictures typical of the far more ambitious subjects Petit starts to draw during this trip.

similar pictures, all part of the intense burst of artistic activity in 1838 when Petit was developing the style he would subsequently use on the Continent. The first two, I think, were drawn from up here.

The landscape is remarkably similar, even now in April 2018 exactly 180 years later. But, while Mayfield church is visible, Ashbourne might not be. It appears only when sunlight reflects off the steeple, causing it suddenly to emerge from the background. It is an astonishing sight if you manage to catch it, and this is what Petit was trying to capture with the rays of light in the first painting, and the steeple dimly shown against the hills beyond in the second.

The third picture is clearly from further away, either in this direction, or perhaps from along the main A515. The fourth picture, remarkable because of the light and the impressionistic trees, is described as Field Norbury, but the view is of Ashbourne and even Mayfield in the distance. This I have not made sense of, because they seem to be too far away to get such a view, at least now.

Landscape painting had been dominated by English artists since the previous century and had gradually become more daring under the influence of Gainsborough, Turner, de Wint, and Constable, to name just a few. The first part of the nineteenth century is sometimes called the golden age of British art and watercolours in particular, a medium that Turner did more than anyone to make a respectable alternative to oil, with its qualities of vibrancy and immediacy to offset what it lacks in permanence. By the middle of the nineteenth century the best English artists were laying

6.3c. Ashbourne and Mayfield, April 1838, 15 × 27. Possibly just one month earlier, with the palette we saw at Ellastone.

6.3d. Field Norbury, May 1838, 30 × 24. Petit's stylistic development seems to have reached this greater vibrancy in May 1838; subsequently he would use it on his trip to France.

the basis of impressionism with the way they managed to communicate the quality of the light and the feel of a scene without much precise detail. This is exactly Petit's approach, with his own special motivation for preservation of heritage, and his very distinctive style.

Along this road, about a mile, opposite a road junction to the left, on the right-hand side is a footpath leading to a bridge over the Dove and on to the stream where I think was the old Mill near Calwich which we will encounter below. Not part of this tour, but pleasant enough on the river bridge.

These are just four of many landscapes painted in this region in the Spring of 1838.

6.4a. St Mary and St Barlock's, Norbury, c. 1838, 19 ×
24. The picture used in *Remarks* is identical save for an
extra window in the nave being included.

6.4aa. Norbury Church, p.102, vol. 2, *Remarks on
Church Architecture.*

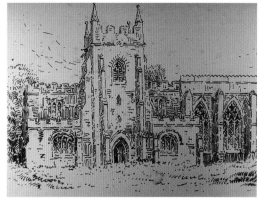

6.4 St Mary and St Barlok, Norbury, Ashbourne de6 2eq

Drive on to the end of Sides Lane, turn right and
then very soon right again to Norbury Manor and Church and park on the circle, shown as 4 on the
map on the following page.

Norbury, and the nearby village of Roston, are both mentioned in the Domesday Book. At one
stage the Manor was owned by a Priory at Tutbury. The Fitzherbert family first rented the estate in
1125, and then acquired it, and kept it until 1872. Many of their tombs and memorials can be seen
in the church.

6.4b. St Mary and St Barlock's, Norbury, c. 1838, 24 × 19. Petit painted the church from every angle, to be sure he would have whatever view he might require.

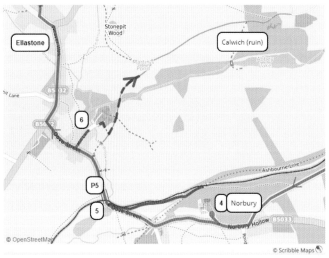

The church itself was mostly built between the fourteenth and sixteenth centuries, yet one can immediately see why Petit admired it and used it in his writings. He devotes a page in the chapter on Form and Proportion to Norbury as an example of how styles have been mixed and combined harmoniously. Petit's comments are worth reading today, because he picks out the details that contribute most, in his opinion, to the overall effect. In Norbury in particular he draws one's attention to:

- the parapet which is not a battlement, but more of a waved line;
- the round-headed windows of the nave, showing how well they can be mixed with more traditional Gothic;

6.4c. Interior, St Mary and St Barlock's, Norbury, c. 1838, 25 × 19. The font and roof, shown here are little changed. The east window was blocked up at the time, as can be seen in this picture.

- the position of the tower, so suitable by comparison with one at the west, in this setting;
- the scale and pinnacles of the tower, not really Gothic (apparently) but fitting perfectly;
- the roses, built into the stone in the side windows, similar to Checkley see Fig. 5.5c;
- and inside, the roof, unbroken by a chancel arch, alabaster monuments and fine woodwork.

It is this precise detailing of the sources of the beauty of a building, combined with his pictures that made Petit so popular as an architectural critic, and which I think we can enjoy today. Notice particularly how the pinnacles so perfectly add to this church tower, compared to Ecclestone, or Sandon at the start of tour 5.

As this edifice crowns a steep wooded bank upon the Dove, and is almost connected with some domestic buildings of nearly the same date and character, it is a very striking object in the scenery of that beautiful district.

The church is as beautiful now as it was then – which is a rare compliment in this book. Petit did about fifteen pictures of the church in and around 1838, to capture every angle and find what would work best. Also shown here, a picture of a lane, that looks to be the road outside the drive, and a slightly damaged one of the village of Norbury, which I have not yet situated, although that building should be distinctive enough.

6.4e. Near Norbury, 1830s, 19 × 27. An earlier picture from near the village.

6.4d. Near Norbury, 1838, 25 × 18. The road close to where the church and manor house stand.

6.5 Ellastone and Norbury from the Dove (same postcode as above)

Very agreeable 20 minute round trip walk from bridge.

Continue down the B5033 to cross the bridge over the river and park as close to it on the other side as you can (see P5 on map). The footpath starts just back before the bridge with steps built into the low brick wall. Following it will lead you to the exact spot where the picture was drawn (roughly two thirds of the way along the blue line) with a view across to Ellastone church, and the Weaver Hills in the distance. The exact spot can be located by seeing where the church stands in relation to the three Weaver Hills. Notice that there is no question of artistic licence, the hills are in the right proportion to each other. The river is, happily, remarkably similar too, quite full and fast flowing in spring.

If you continue along the river, as you come to a small wooden bridge across a tributary stream, you will see Norbury Church above you. The walk is pleasant until the fallen tree, or even a bit further uphill, but after that it reaches a plantation and then the road. It never regains the river.

6.5. Ellaston, 1838, 21 × 27. The view from the River Dove.

6.6a. Ellaston Mill, April 1838, 18 × 23. The house still exists, but now it is somewhat the worse for wear.

6.6 Ellastone Mill, Ellastone de6 2hf

From here take the car on towards the village and take the second right turn, Mill Lane. Park on the side before going too far. At the end, remarkably, you will find the remains of the mill shown in the picture. The original building is still the same, modified and absent the wheel, and of course all the other buildings around have been built. There is a date on the side, 1822,

6.6b. Calwich Abbey, 1820s or 1830s, 11 × 21. A few of these black and white drawings exist, which are hard to date. In some it is clear that Petit aims to capture moonlight (see 7.5).

6.6c. Ford near Calwich Abbey, April 1838, 18 × 25.

which one can just make out. It is unusual to find as much of such a simple mill house at all.

Old simple buildings are called 'vernacular architecture'. The word is also used to describe every-day language as opposed to literary language, and comes from a Latin word for 'domestic' or 'native'. The other mill we saw in tour 3 had been completely rebuilt, and of the one nearby at Calwich, for which there is a picture below, I could find no trace.

A Non-stop: Calwich Abbey and Ford

For those able and wanting to take an extra walk, in addition to the two short walks already taken, there is a path which continues on from Mill Lane, through Dove Farm to Calwich and the two

6.6d. Mill near Calwich, 1830s, 19 × 13. An earlier picture from a location still to be found.

pictures shown here. However the walk is unremarkable, it takes 45 minutes, and the sites of the pictures cannot be reached from the public footpath, which is why it is a very optional extra.

The Priory at Calwich was started around 1130 as an offshoot of Kenilworth Priory and lasted over four hundred years. While it has been described as always having been small and relatively poor, one could also say that its four-hundred years life is not so bad by modern standards. After the Reformation change came frequently. It became a dwelling house, the old priory was demolished, the house built closer to the stream, and the stream dammed up to become a lake. It changed owners several times and was then rebuilt again in 1849–50. So the first picture shows the house before the present one, in moonlight from the river.

The second picture is of a ford across the River Dove just a little further on, where the house is visible on the right, and Ellastone church left of centre too. Unfortunately there is currently no footpath along that part of the Dove on either side.

MYSTERY PICTURE:
MILL NEAR CALWICH

The third picture is a complete mystery. It is clearly not the Mill at Ellastone because of the confluence of streams, so I guess there must have been a mill further on past Calwich Abbey itself. There are a number of houses, and one stream past the ruin, but no location that looks like the picture. The group of houses in Calwich is, in any case, best approached from the pleasant footpath starting on the opposite side of the Dove, on Sides Lane, or by walking down from the Mayfield Road (less interesting but shorter).

6.7a. Ellaston, 1830s, 32 × 24. There is a marked difference between this, conventional, albeit well-drawn, watercolour, and the more interesting (impressionistic/adventurous) drawings of 1838 and 1839.

6.7 Ellastone Church, Ellastone, ST14 5HF

Ellastone (old spelling without the 'e' at the end) is now within walking distance. Here there are two pictures where it is rewarding to find the exact spot. Turn right at the t-junction and then left just after the afore-mentioned Dunscombe Arms. The church is on the right with parking in front.

The tower dates from 1586 and the church itself from various earlier periods. More recently the nave was rebuilt in 1830 and, some time after this picture was drawn, probably in the early 1840s, the pinnacles on the tower were removed. This is worth noticing. In this instance the church tower seems to look good with or without pinnacles. To see where the picture was drawn from we will want the narrow lane running alongside, past the church and just before the bend.

Petit chose a view where the rest of the church besides the tower is not visible, and at least so far as I have found, devoted practically no time to it by comparison with Norbury, Ashbourne and Mayfield earlier on this tour, or Leigh and Checkley in tour 5. Almost certainly that is because of the nave being rebuilt just previously, destroying the character of the medieval one. Is that a bit harsh after a further 150 years?

The next picture is at the end of the lane which is one minute by car down the main Ribden road, or a walk along the lane. Go to the entrance to the field on the south corner of Church lane and the main road (b on map). The second picture is a view of the Weaver Hills similar to the view here, perhaps from a little further

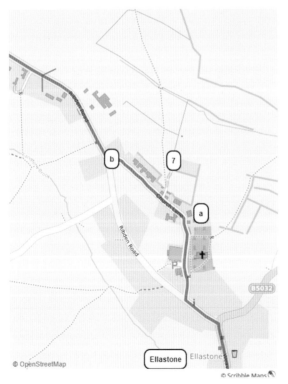

6.7b. Ellaston, 1838, 14 × 24. In fact a view of the Weaver Hills from somewhere in or near Ellastone (the 'e' at the end seems to have been at best optional, 180 years ago).

back. It is quite likely that it is not the right spot because the middle hill looks a bit higher in the picture although not in reality, but it is the best I have found so far.

Could Petit have tampered with the scene to create a better picture, as artists did? There were by then two rather distinct strands of topographical painters. Those who carefully stuck to the facts, and those who felt free to amend what they saw in order either (cynically) to make a saleable picture or (romantically) to convey the feeling they wanted to express. Turner is usually credited with the extreme development of the latter trend although he could be accurate too. The antiquarians and travellers often wanted faithful copies because photography and postcards had not quite made it yet.

Petit is unusual in that he tried to do both – be accurate, yet convey the effect of the scene or building. So I am inclined to think I might not have found the right place, unless this was a rare exception.

6.8 GREENS HILL, WOOTTON, DE6 2GW

1.5 miles north along Ribden Road, and three minutes at most by car. Go into the village of Wootton and at the sharp bend turn right and then left into the old village. You want the high point, between the old red telephone kiosk (now a book deposit) and the old post box with a plant inside, near the start of Salts Lane. Although the view of the hills is partially blocked by a house, this is where this rather bleak picture was drawn, I would say.

6.8. Weaver Hills, April 1838, 13 × 23. From the village, from one of the two albums made in this region between March and May 1838.

Wootton used to be called Wootton under Weaver, and in the past it had a reputation as a fairly bleak place, belonging to the squire of Wootton Lodge, nearby, which we visited at the end of tour 5. In 1831 the population was claimed to be 269, with twenty families warranting a listing by virtue of their independent occupations. Half of them were farmers, and half in the most important trades

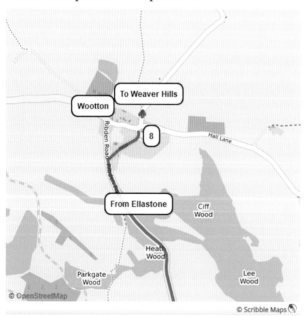

one would expect to find: two blacksmiths, a saddler, a shoemaker, a wheelwright, a shopkeeper, a schoolmaster, a victualler and a tailor who also doubled as a second shop-keeper. Five families had the surname Salt so hardly surprising that there is a Salts Lane here. According to the 1834 *Gazetteer* 'the inhabitants formerly described the wildness of this moorland district by the following distich [rhyme]: "Wootton Under Weaver, where God came never". So the village looks a lot more prosperous now, albeit no shops or blacksmiths still operating.

In the 1830s Ellastone had a hundred more inhabitants than Wootton, with thirty tradesmen listed, including four more Salts, two of whom ran the two pubs. But

Ellastone was the centre of its own parish. It seems to have thrived much better than its neighbour over the years.

If you have time continue directly in the direction of sight and drive up onto the Weaver Hills which we have been gradually approaching. It is open courtesy of the Wootton estate. The Bamfords, owners of Wootton Lodge, which we saw at the end of tour 5, are welcoming here. On a fine day the views are spectacular, and on a bad day this picture will make perfect sense.

Tour 7

Dovedale: Nature as God's Work

Petit's earliest landscapes record the hills and valleys of his native Staffordshire, and a little across the border into Derbyshire. The majority of this tour are of these scenes, although we start, and finish, with simple and largely unspoilt parish churches. The exact dates of all the pictures are not known, but judging by how Petit's style evolved in the early and mid-1830s some of these could be from the 1820s, when he was assistant curate in Lichfield, or from his earlier student days, while only one seems after 1840. They came from four different albums, so it might have been a regular holiday spot during those days.

Dovedale itself is a major attraction, with tourists visiting all the places listed in this tour. But in the off season you will find about the same number of visitors as Petit likely found. The difference is that almost no-one paints these days. By the 1830s, landscape visiting had long been an established pastime, and not only for the wealthy. Painting picturesque landscapes was the profession of a few, but the occupation of very many as a way of being in and enjoying nature, not just because they did not have digital cameras.

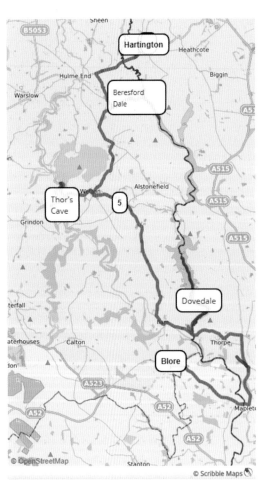

The pictures are interesting because they are the furthest away from Petit's architectural sketches – his dramatic representations of churches such as we saw in Wolverhampton, or the later quite reddish sketches such as of Lichfield in the last tour. In some ways these are more conventional.

In the eighteenth century, topographical pictures could be a little dull and stiff. Then Cozens and especially Turner led the way for most of the first half of the nineteenth century, developing techniques to convey the emotion of the scene. Petit would have been aware of this trend and follows it. He was clearly talented even by the 1820s, but not as distinctively powerful as he would become later, in works such as the picture of Ilam Rock (7.4) the one later picture from the 1840s, when he ranks among the best topographical artists of his generation.

7.1. Blore Church, 1820s, 19 × 13. A very simple small picture, with little of the character Petit would later develop.

To get to all the places shown here, one needs walking boots, and all of a day. Indeed to take a room in one of the local B&Bs, or if you can manage it in the Izaak Walton Hotel (see 7.3), would be rewarding. However, for the less abled, even driving as close as one can will show Staffordshire at its best, and far better than it is ever given credit for.

7.1 St Bartholemew, Blore, Ashbourne, de6 2bs

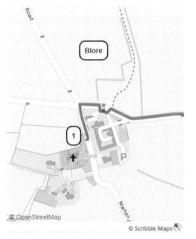

We start at Blore, and its eleventh-century church in a beautiful village overlooking the Dove valley after it exits from the gorge that is Dovedale. All the roads to Blore are attractive drives.

A very small picture, it is shown at actual size here. In style it is conventional, not reflecting the individuality that Petit was to develop later, and it does not do full justice to the church. This remained unchanged, without Victorian restoration, until repairs and renovations in the 1990s, which did not alter the character. This, as you will know by now, is a fortunate rarity.

The exact spot where the picture was drawn is the far corner of the churchyard. You will see that the tree in the picture has been replaced by a younger one in the same place. Only the old weather vane on top of the tower is no longer there. The village is also about the same size as it was then, just a few houses around Blore Hall, which is now owned by a holiday property company.

I am not aware of Petit drawing Blore during his extended visit to the region in 1838, although in general the humble parish church was as much in his mind as the grander cathedral – as, in fairness, it was for most architectural commentators of whatever side in Victorian times.

7.2. Thorpe Cloud, 1830s, 9 × 22. An early Petit watercolour – contrast with 7.3

7.2 THORPE CLOUD (1), SPEND LANE, ASHBOURNE, DE6 2AS

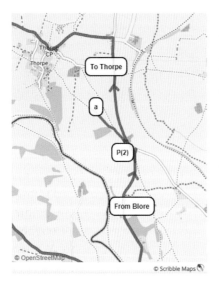

Thorpe is only three miles and ten minutes away, just over the border in Derbyshire – the border is the river Dove. The main road to Dovedale can be busy, especially at weekends, but the village is peaceful. The first spot is best approached via Mapleton.

Neither picture is in fact of the village of Thorpe; they show different views of the well-known mountain – well, peak – called Thorpe Cloud, that lies above the village. The first picture was taken from a footpath that starts on Spend Lane, just after a left turn (heading towards Thorpe) as you come up the road from Mapleton. The view from the road is similar. To find the right spot you should follow the footpath through the gap in the stone wall into the second field and a further 100 yards on. The building shown in the dip between the two hills may not be Thorpe church, but the top of the old farmhouse.

7.3 THORPE CLOUD (2), IZAAK WALTON HOTEL, DE6 2AY

The second picture, drawn I believe a few years later, shows a completely different side of Thorpe Cloud. It can equally well be visited after Dovedale.

The picture was painted from the end of the patio along the side of the Izaak Walton Hotel (where the bar serves coffee, tea and meals all day) The scene is as remarkable now as it was then, and if you get the view from the hotel on a sunny day it will be one of the most beautiful in the whole book. Best of all is to stay the night in any of rooms 22 to 26, because the extra height helps. The end of

7.3. Thorpe Cloud, c. 1836, 23 × 32. Tackling the same subject much more ambitiously, and effectively.

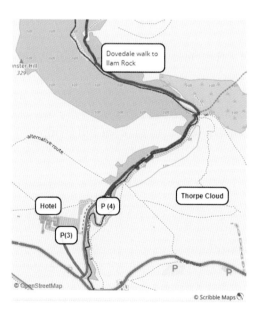

the hotel is newish and it is not clear if Petit was in a previous structure or at ground level. The hotel website records that it is on the site of a seventeenth-century inn or guesthouse and was active as such throughout the nineteenth century, which is confirmed by William White's 1834 Gazette. Izaak Walton and his fishing book were already famous by then. Unfortunately there are no records with the current hotel owners from that time that might record if Petit stayed here.

7.4 ILAM ROCK, DOVEDALE, DE6 2AY (CAR PARK) Long, flat and beautiful walk

These pictures can only be reached by hiking about forty-five minutes from the Dovedale car park (200 metres down the side-road beyond the hotel entrance),

7.4a. Ilam Rock, c. 1843. 34 × 26. Petit was to write about landscape as God's work, and from the 1840s on he would convey a spiritual aspect in many landscapes, hinted at here.

or coming from the other direction, downstream from Milldale. If you are in a party with two cars, take one up to Milldale first.

Petit painted in Dovedale on at least three occasions, which implies that he made several visits, equipped with sketching materials. The first shown is the last, and best, picture, painted in about 1844, after the rest of those on this tour. It is one of his most finished landscapes of the period, and might have been worked up in the studio, because to get the range of colouring shown in a sketch on the spot would be quite a feat.

7.4b. Dovedale, 1830s, 19 × 14, In contrast this and the next picture are far less ambitious.

7.4c. Dovedale, 1820s, 11 × 7.

In a poem, *The Greater and Lesser Light*, published after his death by his sister, Petit tries to reconcile science with religion. One might suppose he felt some conflict between the scientific method which drove his approach to architecture, and his religious training. Petit argues for the existence of God based on the incredible beauty and variety of nature:

> What! Shall we own the written witness true
> And not the record of creation too?
> Are they but freaks of chance or toys designed
> To cheat and dazzle some enquiring mind?

Darwin had published *On the Origin of Species* in 1859, and it was as controversial then as it is in the Bible Belt of the USA now. Interestingly, according to his sister's introduction, Petit believed the subject could best be tackled in verse rather than prose.

As early as 1841, in his first book, Petit refers to nature as God's work, in contrast to architecture as man's work. For him the infinite variety and beauty of nature is both a challenge and an inspiration to architects to strive for something original that would stand the test of time. This picture of Ilam Rock has much in common with some of his church pictures.

If you manage to get there you can find pretty much the exact spot that it was drawn from, on the opposite side of the river from the main path, looking back to the rock downstream, where you can see the valley to the left of the rock.

The second picture from this group, a smaller, earlier, rough sketch I had thought inaccurate until I found the spot, because of the odd angles of the two rocks in upper left centre. However go back downstream past the first jutting rock close to the path. This has a plaque on it to a father and son who aided the establishment of the park. A bit further downstream is the spot, looking back towards Ilam Rock. It is remarkable how accurate it is. The only problem is the height of the two rocks, and I think Petit must have sat higher up the bank, but it was raining too heavily for me at the time to resolve that. The third picture appears to be the same rock from near where Ilam is.

7.5. Near Alstonefield, 1820s or 1830s, 6.5 × 13. As we saw at Calwich Abbey, a rare picture done to capture the effect of the scene in moonlight.

Sketching from nature, as it was called, was partly an exercise in logistics. One needed a portable easel to hold the paper, as well as deciding exactly what colours and brushes one would take, and then organising it all in a satchel. A source of water nearby was very helpful. Being an obsessive sketcher, known for completing up to four in one day in later life, as opposed to the usual one or two, Petit had this down to a tee and apparently had a satchel specially designed for the bits he took.

7.5 Near Alstonefield, Ashbourne, de6 2fr

Next a fifteen-minute car journey up the valley to Alstonefield. The road goes through Ilam village, winner of lots of competitions, with a beautiful Youth Hostel/Park/Old Mansion house, run as a partnership between the National Trust and the Youth Hostels Association. There is a medieval church in the grounds. However, I have not yet found a picture by Petit of somewhere in Ilam village, it is unlikely that he passed over it altogether.

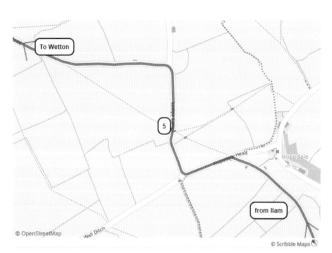

This small, and rather unusual picture of a wanderer in the gleam of moonlight near Alstonefield was actually taken between Alstonefield and Wetton. At the junction reached a couple of miles after leaving Ilam turn left to Wetton, not right

7.6a. Wetton Dale and Thor's Cave, 1830s, 23 × 332. Showing the old Gretton Church in the distance. Petit visited this spot several times in the 1830s.

to Alstonefield, and round the first right-hand bend is a footpath crossing the road. The barn shown in the picture is still there, set at the right position against Wetton Hill beyond.

Going by Petit's later verse, the moonlit scene is not intended to be gloomy, but through its unusual beauty, inviting:

> Far o'er the waste His hospitable light
> Gleams, not to warn or threaten, but invite;
> His call is heard, to welcome and to press
> The weary stranger from the wilderness,
> Or gently win with love's persuasive voice
> The blinded wand'rer to his better choice.

In 1831 the parish of Alstonefield had a population of 650, including a good inn for tourists, now called The George, so not much different from today; there was also a large workhouse for the poor of surrounding parishes who would break stones and prepare marble slabs from a quarry at Wetton.

7.6b. Wetton Dale and Thor's Cave, 1830s, 27 × 19. The river and sun shafts seem to create a better balanced picture than the others.

7.6 Wetton Dale and Thor's Cave, Wetton, Ashbourne, de6 2af

One minute further on lies the village of Wetton. Turn left after the pub, and go past the church, straight on down the valley. On the left are the best views of Thor's cave from the road. About two-hundred yards on there is a footpath on the right where two field gates meet the road (p on map). Take this footpath, keeping left through the second gate. In Petit's day it seems Thor's cave was at least as popular as Ilam Rock, and equally inaccessible, perhaps that is less true now when far more people go to Dovedale. However most people have a mixed reaction to these pictures. Somehow the gaping black hole does not look good in a picture, which may explain the many attempts, of which three are shown. The first (on the previous page), I think was painted as you come around the side of a tangle of undergrowth. The road probably did not exist, and the footpath, which followed the road until the gates, was the main route into the valley. The walk is only five minutes, but can be muddy if wet.

The old church of Grindon, visible in the distance in Fig. 7.6a, was demolished in 1845, and replaced by the one with the spire that you see now, in conformity with Ecclesiologist 'principles'.

Since we are doing poetry on this tour, this is what Petit added into *Remarks* in 1841 about reconstruction and destructive restoration, introducing the reaction of a person, perhaps a war veteran, returning to his village home after many years, without family, and looking in vain for the church as the symbol of that home:

> …Are those the hallowed walls
> Is that the cherish'd monument of years?
> Lo! in its place a glaring fabric rears
> Its cumbrous front – Ah me, hath modern taste
> The simpler beauties of the fane defac'd
> Hath cold presumptuous art essay'd to hide
> Religion's offering in a mask of pride?

The cave has been a well-known site in the region for ever, but it was harder to reach in Petit's day. This path might have been the main route between the village and valley before the road was built.

7.6c. Wetton Dale and Thor's Cave, 1830s, 14 × 19. From further back, a slightly damaged picture but showing the old mill in the valley (now a café).

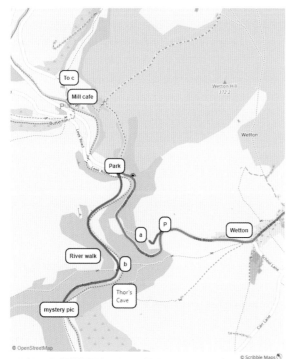

Back on the road, at the bottom is a car park (Park on the map), and a flat ten-minute walk to the bottom of Thor's cave, along the old Leek–Manifold Light Railway line which was in operation from 1904 to 1934. Remarkably this was and had been a mining region, trekking out copper ore from under the nearby Ecton Hill, to the enrichment of the Duke of Devonshire, Chatsworth, and the Crescent at Buxton. Although there is no sign of this industry in Petit's pictures.

If you walk down the valley, when you arrive close to the cave, there is a tourist information board, and a bridge, on the other side of which I think Petit painted the second picture. There

7.6d. 'Narrow Dale', 1838, 25 × 20. Not Narrow Dale, quite possibly further downstream in Wetton Dale, looking back to the cave outcrop.

are direct footpaths down from the village to the cave or to the bridge but these are steeper than walking along the valley. Reaching the cave is slippery in the wet.

Along the road half a mile north, at the top of the map, is Wetton Mill and café, which is seen in the third picture from above, a very recent discovery. To get there one should take the footpath which starts just past the mill, which I have yet to do. A little further down the valley from the cave is my favoured site for the mystery picture (see map).

MYSTERY PICTURE

This picture is labelled Narrow dale, as is another one in Wolfscotedale. But it is not in the current Narrowdale, Wolfscotedale, Beresford Dale, or north of Hartington to Pilsbury. One possibility might be along Dovedale, before Ilam Rock, but the trees are too thick to say. My best guess is that the scene is here in Wetton Dale, past Thor's Cave, looking back to that rock formation from 200 yards downstream.

Going back to the poem, Petit's second argument, also from nature, was the existence of a remarkable sense of harmony and beauty that, by and large, we share.

> Surely some sense, mysterious, undefined
> Pervades the deep recesses of the mind
> 'Twere hard to say, of which objects given to sight
> Why this offends and that affords delight
> And harmony, proportion, beauty rest
> On some obscure, inexplicable test.

For Petit there was no formula for the forms and proportions of beauty, such as those that early architects had proposed. For him beauty, harmony and proportion had to be sensed, although the proportions of the best examples achieved to date should be studied. Hence his empirical approach of drawing and presenting lots of beautiful examples.

Notice that where you park the car there is water in the river bed, but not here, except when very wet, as in the picture. Close around the car park it disappears into tunnels and reemerges near Ilam.

7.7a. Beresford Dale, 1838. Courtesy of Staffordshire County Museum Service. Not surprisingly this picture appears to come from the same journey as (b) which is dated.

7.7 BERESFORD DALE AND WOLFSCOTEDALE, BERESFORD LANE, SK17 0HQ
Two walks, 30 minutes and 45 minutes

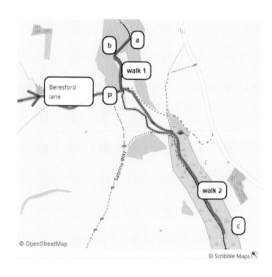

Follow the road to Hartington, then turn off for Beresford Dale and Beresford Lane. The road winds past a couple of caravan parks to the river. From here take the footpath to the left along the river bank. This part of the Dove valley is called Beresford Dale. The walk is short – fifteen minutes – and very pleasant. The first picture is around the big right-hand bend, you will see the strange rocky outcrop which still stands exactly as it was 170 years ago, and you can find the spot of the picture.

The second picture is harder. The best likeness is from this side of the little bridge, looking back downstream. It appears that the far bank has changed. It might have been altered when the regular little weirs were put in the stream to reduce erosion of the bed, and presumably to aid fishing.

The walk through the gorge continues for a further ten minutes until it opens out and it is all worthwhile. If you do walk further on, high up on the left cliff is Beresford Hall. This was noted in the 1834 *Gazette* as being an ancient manor dating back to William the Conqueror.

Retrace your steps back down river for another walk, which while all right, is not as good as the first. Past Beresford Lane, across the footbridge (into Derbyshire again), the river enters what is now called Wolfscotedale. In Petit's day this appears to have been called Narrowdale – the name that is now given just to the side valley to the right, which definitely does not contain the pictured scene.

Continue along Wolfescotedale and the picture appears to me to be about a mile downstream, when the hills fall into the shape shown. Now the river is tamer and the hill covered in green, probably because twenty-first-century winters are much milder. This was quite a way to carry one's

7.7b. Beresford Dale, 1838, 20 ×
26.

7.7c. 'Narrow Dale' 1838, 18 ×
26. This is not the location that
we currently name Narrow Dale
either; but more likely along
Wolfescote Dale beside the main
River Dove.

watercolour kit, as we saw at Ilam Rock too. Unless you are in a party with two cars, it is necessary to retrace one's steps, but the walks both ways are good.

7.8 St Giles, Hartington, Buxton, sk17 0ar

Returning back to the car in Beresford Lane, one then takes a couple of right turns heading north and a little east to arrive at the historic, now tourist, village of Hartington, just over the border into Derbyshire again. Here we end the tour with a picture of a notable parish church. The picture was drawn from the south side. One can see some changes added since, such as pinnacles to the transept roof, but, importantly, the sturdy and protective character of the church, derived from its elevated position above the village, is unchanged.

7.8. St Giles Church, Hartington, c. 1839, 21 × 26. An architectural sketch designed to show the 'western tower of good design, and very large transepts'.

7.8. Hartington Church, p. 96, vol. 2, *Remarks on Church Architecture*

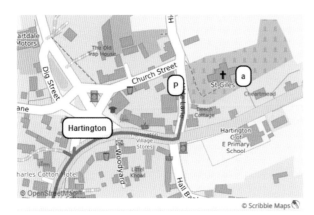

Petit includes the church in his first book, in the chapter on Form and Proportion, because of its unusually large transepts – the side extensions to the north and south; which 'give it a peculiar character and the inside spacious and convenient.' However, I will end with a quote from his speech 'On the Principles of Gothic Architecture as Applied to Parish Churches' delivered at Oxford in 1846 and subsequently published as a book. Petit was invited to address one of the two most influential societies which had until then advocated the use of gothic. The Oxford Society had not been as aggressive as the Cambridge one, and contained some strong Petit supporters. Of course he used the opportunity to argue against any rule or standard, especially for the simpler parish churches:

> By framing our ideas of fitness according to one arbitrary standard, we shall lose the perception of that beautiful variety which pervades the whole range of Christian architecture; we shall learn to criticize, where a correcter taste and a more just impulse prompt us to admire; we shall become insensible to the solemnity of some of our ecclesiastical structures, when we ought to be able to recognize, even in the simple village church, the development of an art, grounded on the firmest principles…

It basically advocates, yet again, conserving our wonderful variety of styles and not accepting arbitrary rules on what is correct architecture: equally applicable today.

Tour 8

In Lichfield: Home

This tour is best done on foot; the total distance is about two and a half miles, with plenty of nice stops along the way. Alternatively one could walk just in the vicinity of the Cathedral and visit the other spots by car afterwards.

Parking for the Cathedral is best found opposite the entrance to the close in Beacon Street Car Park, WS13 6PZ (marked P to the left of point 3 on the overview map). There are bigger busier car parks between the Cathedral and the town centre. If you park here, start in Beacon Park before crossing the road and entering the Cathedral close.

Lichfield is a city that is still dominated by its Cathedral. With hills from the north round to the south-east there are great views of the Cathedral's spires from many angles. Petit was brought up not far from Lichfield, and his mother moved the family here in 1823 after his father died. Petit himself moved back to it in 1845. From then until the end of his life it was his main home.

The Cathedral seems to have been a never-ending source of inspiration for him, especially how the three spires look from different angles and different distances, and in all seasons and weathers. He painted it more than a hundred times during the course of his life, and it is likely that more than fifty of those have survived. Painting the Cathedral seems to have acted like a centre of gravity to which he would always return. While earlier drawings are architectural and from close in, later he seems to have used it to experiment with different effects, different types of view and weather conditions, and perhaps it was a form of relaxation.

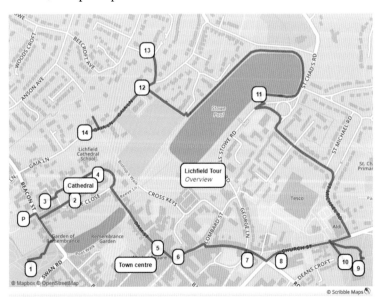

142

8.1. Lichfield from Beacon Park, c. 1860, 26 × 37, the Ian Cooke Collection. One of the later landscape pictures of the Cathedral that he painted from every angle over the years. A rare one in sunshine.

Petit's pictures of Lichfield are especially significant within the body of his later work (after 1848). Although the subject is in one sense the same, as art they all different. In this book there are few other examples of his later work because in later life Petit travelled more outside the county and abroad rather than in Staffordshire. He was painting prolifically after 1850, but mostly architectural sketches to support his speeches and his articles for his battles with the Gothicists. Completed pictures done mainly for art's sake, like those of Lichfield, are relatively rare.

Here we select views that form a circle, starting and finishing at the parking place shown. For convenience and because the scale allows, each picture is separately numbered on the overview map. While there are some earlier pictures, mainly closer in, there are half a dozen middle distance views from the 1850s and 1860s which capture the different moods and colours of Lichfield and demonstrate Petit's later art.

8.1 Beacon Park (south west view) ws13 6qz

The first of the later pictures just mentioned, this one is remarkable for its bright, summery atmosphere, well suited to the modern-day Beacon Park.

The site from which Petit painted this picture seems to be well back inside the park, behind the fountain. The building with the cupola on the corner of the roof is unchanged and this will allow you to find more or less the exact spot, perhaps near the statue. The cow is unlikely to be seen, however, it is the three steeples and their relationship with each other that are the things to notice here and later.

The statue in the modern park, erected in the twentieth century, is to Captain Smith of the Titanic. He is described in heroic terms on the plaque, because he went down with the ship: not at all the impression given by modern films. This may seem a bit of a tangent, but it serves as an example of the way reputations rise or fall over time. In Petit's case, from being genuinely heroic in his lifetime (by virtue of steadfastly sticking to what he felt – and what we would feel – is right, in the face of often grossly unfair criticism). His reputation was traduced by Scott and the Gothicists after his death and only now can it be recovered.

Now return across Bird Road, into the Cathedral Close and walk up to the west front.

8.2–4 The Cathedral Close, WS13 7LD

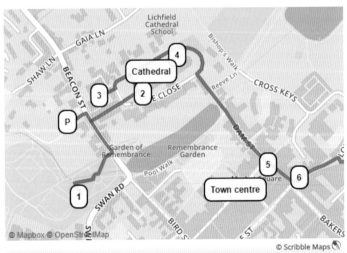

First, a small picture from about 1834, probably a fragment reduced at the top by damage, is a rare image of how the West Front looked before Gilbert Scott's renovation, which began in 1857. The Cathedral's literature is full of praise for Scott's contributions, and by this time Scott had moved from his very pro-Ecclesiological stance of the 1840s to a more independent and original position. The West Front that you see is claimed to be one of his finest achievements. During the eighteenth century the ornaments had been removed and some of the crumbling stonework covered by cement to prevent further deterioration, so one would imagine even Petit might have approved of this renovation.

8.2a. Part of the West Front, c. 1836, 14 × 20. This captures part of the façade before renovation.

8.3. The Cathedral Close, c. 1845, 25 × 20, courtesy of the Samuel Johnson Birthplace Museum, Lichfield. A rare picture where the Cathedral provides the backdrop, as opposed to being the main focus.

Scott's internal alterations, however, we can guess Petit did not approve of. One of the diarists of the age, Augustus Hare, records, in 1862:

> I had a capital sight of the Cathedral with [Petit], beautiful still, though sadly 'jemmyfied' [crammed in] by Scott, who has added some immense statues in the choir, which put everything out of proportion, and has put up a bastard-gothic metal screen.

In Stafford (Tour 2) we saw Scott's external alterations to St Mary's in the 1840s that Petit actively opposed. By the mid-1850s the two were the most prominent advocates of the pro- and anti-Gothic parties, with some spiteful letters written by Scott in *The Builder* answered with pained politeness by Petit. History was subsequently written by the one who lived longer, as is often the case.

The Close includes those alleys to the north-west of the Cathedral that in Petit's day used to be houses in the gift of the Bishop, and now are very well kept. Often these dwellings were let by the Cathedral on peppercorn rents to widows of churchmen or Cathedral employees.

Petit's father was a clergyman in the nearby parish of Shareshill, however they were comfortable enough to own an important house in Tamworth Street, and this was Petit's home until he left to be

8.4. The Chapter House, c. 1843, 24 × 20.

8.4a. Interior, Lichfield Cathedral, 1857, 38 × 27. This shows the poor state of some of the interior, behind the curtain, before restoration.

curate at Bradfield (Essex) in 1828, and again after he returned to live in Lichfield in 1845. It is very likely that he would have known all the residents of the Close.

If you are lucky, while walking in the close or around the Cathedral you may see the pair of peregrine falcons that have taken up residence, presumably in one of the spires. The great advantage of such residents, besides their acrobatics, is keeping down pigeons.

This picture of the Close (Fig. 8.3), is hard to date though it is likely to have been done sometime during the 1840s. It, and a few others from this tour, is on display in the Samuel Johnson Museum on the corner of the Market Square over the bridge in the town, where we go soon. Just behind is the herb garden of Erasmus Darwin's house, Charles Darwin's grandfather being another famous Lichfieldian.

The Chapter House (Fig. 8.4), is to be found at the north-east corner of the Cathedral. This probably dates from the 1840s. It is, by contrast with the West Front, unchanged as you will see, but while this is being written in 2018 there is restoration work going on.

The next picture, of the interior, un-numbered on the map, was drawn in 1857, and shows the damage to the north transept arch and pillar just prior to restoration. Such repair work is exactly what Petit believed restoration should focus on. This picture seems to have been made to record the condition of the building before work began.

8.5. The Cathedral from the town, c. 1842, 27 × 22, the Ian Cooke Collection.
Both this and the following picture, like the one from the Close, show people
and town detail, rare for Petit. Later he would focus on ambitious impressions
of light and effect.

Opposite, in the south transept, in the corner closest to the west side, is a full-length brass memorial to Colonel Peter John Petit, who died in February 1852. Peter was Petit's second and last brother to die. Petit himself was childless so this death must have been an even greater tragedy for the family as it meant that the male Petit line was doomed to end. Petit's pictures from this time are full of frustration and gloom – see 8.13 below and Bilston the first in chapter 4.

The Chapter House café in the south-east corner of the Close offers a simple and pleasant cup of coffee, or lunch. Then take Dam Street into town, around the corner from the cafe.

8.5–8 Town Centre, WS13 6LA

8.6. The Cathedral from the town, c. 1842, 27 × 22, the Ian Cooke Collection.

After reaching the Market Square, walk to the far side of it for the next picture, and a little further to the corner of Tamworth Street for the one after. Both probably date from the early 1840s.

This is also a convenient moment to pop into the Samuel Johnson Museum on the south-west corner of Market Square, located under the word 'centre' on the map on p.140.

Since most of Petit's art only became public thirty years ago, it will, no doubt, take a few more years for him to achieve his rightful position and a museum to himself either in Lichfield or elsewhere. So for the time being Samuel Johnson kindly devotes a little wall space in his museum, where there are five pictures hanging, the only Petits on permanent public display at the time of writing.

Stored (and available to be seen by appointment) in the archives of the museum is an album that once belonged to Petit's sister Emma. It includes the first documented examples of watercolours by his various sisters and his wife, confirmed by initials marked on the mounts. Many less-good watercolours that have been attributed to Petit on eBay and elsewhere are in fact by his sisters. This album, donated anonymously, and preserved in this museum well before much was known about Petit, has been an invaluable help in unravelling the confusion surrounding the Petit family and their circle.

From the town centre, follow Tamworth Street up the gradual hill.

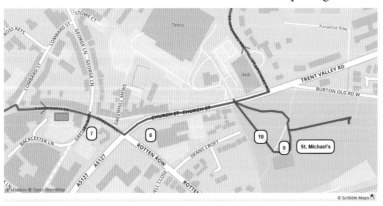

The Petits lived in a big house called Redcourt which used to stand in its garden, with gatehouse and a couple of cottages, where the car park now is (green rectangle on map) before you reach point 7. John Louis returned there in 1845, inherited the family house from his mother in 1852, and lived

8.7. The Cathedral from Gresley Row, or just possibly from his own house, Redcourt, 1857, 27 × 38. A good example of how the town detail is no longer of great interest, Petit's focus is on the effect of the Cathedral in relation to the town.

there, as well as in Longdon (see Tour 1) until his death in 1868. After that it went to the three sisters who lived with him, and when they died in the 1890s his nephew inherited and sold it.

Augustus Hare notes '[Petit] lived in a house built by Miss Porter, Dr Johnson's stepdaughter. With him reside his three sisters and seven cats who appeared at all meals as part of the family... Mr Petit was most extraordinary, but a very interesting companion.'

Petit had six sisters in total, all younger than him; they all painted with varying degrees of proficiency. As we saw in tour 1, it was Emma, the fourth, who accompanied him everywhere and organised his work. For an example of her art see see Fig. 9.15 on p.167.

All Petit's pictures and papers were carefully maintained by his sisters until their deaths in the 1890s, and then less well cared for by a nephew and grandniece until the 1950s. When she died, the hoard of pictures was abandoned; discovered by new owners who, not recognizing their importance, sold off those they could via a regional auctioneer, throwing away those too damaged. Nothing has been heard or seen of the papers. By then no one knew of their existence.

Walk up Tamworth Street until the crossroad of George Lane, and on the right Gresley Row. The views back to the Cathedral from Tamworth Street are blocked, but along Gresley Row, just past the corner building the view is good and the angle and distance both seem right for Fig. 8.7 above,

8.8. The Cathedral from Church Street, c. 1848. This picture was drawn about ten years before the previous one, but five years later than the town views. Although it is badly damaged, and perhaps left unfinished, it reflects a mid point between the two approaches.

made in 1857. This could well have been drawn from a window or garden in his house which you are overlooking as you look across the car park. We certainly lost something in this particular property development, however necessary.

To my mind Fig. 8.7 is the second of the great pictures of the chapter. Compare this with any professional artist of the time, and it captures the atmosphere, and the character of the Cathedral and its relationship with the city, without artifice, and without looking old fashioned and quaint as many Victorian watercolourists can do. However, Petit's pictures are drawn also with the purpose of illustrating the exceptional beauty of the cathedral from every angle. In a speech 'On Principles and Prejudices in Architecture' he says:

> As an instance of fine proportion, I will notice Lichfield Cathedral, in relation of the three steeples to each other, to the respective spaces that separate them, and to the height and length of the whole building. Neither the length of the nave, nor its height, nor the size and height of the towers and spires, nor the distance between the western spires, seem to have been determined by any rules of construction or convenience; there appears to be no reason why the forms and proportions should not be altered ad libitum [as one wishes]. Yet we feel that any addition to the length of the nave, any heightening of any one of the towers, any material alteration in their bulk, or in the distance between them, or in the height of the nave itself, would infallibly destroy the beauty of the building...

I do not know how this Gresley Row came to be so named. The Gresleys were a large Derbyshire family and Petit became closely related to them. We encountered them in tour 3 at their home in Netherseale. Petit's wife's younger sister, Georgina, married the Gresley who later became head of

8.9. The Porch, St Michael's, Greenhill, c. 1828, 16 × 24. Although early, yet the picture shows an unconventional angle, typical of Petit.

the family and inherited a baronetcy. Another Gresley was living in the Cathedral Close and contributing to the Anastatic Drawing Society albums mentioned.

Now return to the crossroad, and walk uphill, just across the main road, Church Street. Fig. 8.8 was drawn here, where you can see a gap between the Cathedral and the Chinese restaurant.

Why include a damaged, near-ruined, example of an artist whose achievements have yet to be appreciated? A second one in fact, for we have already encountered the one at Bilston, the first picture in Tour 4. That one had historic significance, while this is just a great picture that would have been. The current estimate is that at least one third of Petit's work was lost to damage between the time of his sisters' deaths and the moment when the remains of his work were consigned to auctions en masse. This picture is a reminder of what is tragically lost, ruined or destroyed prematurely.

8.9–10 To St Michael's, ws13 6ed

Walk along Church Street for a couple of hundred yards, which soon brings you to the entrance to the ancient churchyard of St Michael's, on the right. The first picture is a view of the side entrance of the church, from a funny angle. It was painted much earlier than the previous pictures we have seen on this tour except perhaps the small view of Lichfield West Front.

Petit worked as assistant curate at St Michael's after taking holy orders in 1825, before heading off to Bradfield, Essex, as curate in 1828. This picture could have been drawn during his time working here or a little later, but before 1835.

It is quite hard to imagine the competition for priestly work in those days, but it must have been similar to that for professional work today. The starting point was assistant curate, which was a bit like an internship, and then curate where you did all the work for the incumbent vicar for a minimal wage, while the vicar took the bulk of the 'living'. Families pulled strings, as they do today, to get their sons onto this ladder, and I would guess Petit's was no different – anyway he found his initial footing close to home, in one of the most beautiful parish settings.

8.10. The Cathedral from St Michael's, 1857, 27 × 37. This picture was drawn just a couple of months before the one at 8.7 above in January of 1857.

Turn back to see the Cathedral and somewhere close by is the exact spot where Petit sat to make this next picture. The third of the later atmospheric views (Fig. 8.10), it was also painted in 1857.

St Michael's has an extraordinary history. The churchyard has yielded flints dating from the Mesolithic period (i.e. pre-farming, around 5,000 BC in this part of the world) and burial remains from Saxon times. It is claimed to be one of the five most important ancient burial grounds in England, which might be what drew St Chad to Lichfield in the seventh century.

While the church in its current shape dates from 1190, most of the building was 'restored' in the 1840s and the medieval character entirely lost. Petit almost certainly painted the rest of the church before this but the only work to have come to light so far is the one shown here. He probably did not paint it afterwards, but continued to come to the churchyard to enjoy the view.

If you visit when the church is open, inside facing the congregation from behind the pulpit on the left is a memorial plaque to Petit's uncle. A little incongruous in that position. Louis Hayes Petit died aged 74 after a career as a barrister until 1821 and then MP for the pocket borough of Ripon between 1827 and 1832 – until apparently disagreeing with the seat's patron over the Reform Bill which he supported. There is a picture of him in the National Portrait Gallery.

John Louis Petit is buried in the churchyard, in a family vault, together with six of his siblings. All

8.11. The Cathedral from Stowe Pool, 1857, 27 × 37. Also from the winter of 1857, however here Petit is concerned to capture the excavation of Stowe Pool by the new water authority.

the old gravestones were moved around in the late 1960s and this accounts for the jumbled smaller tombstones clustered under the trees beyond the immediate vicinity of the church, nevertheless, perhaps because of its size, the Petit vault has survived. There are other even bigger vaults in the churchyard, the most notable being to former chancellor of Lichfield James Thomas Law which you pass just on the left after the main entrance to the grounds.

To get to the Petit vault from the church entrance facing the road, follow the path to the right and parallel to the road. This leads to the modern graveyard, but just before the division there is a large tomb with four corner pillars and the Petit vault is behind it.

Petit's inscription, on the side facing the path, is in Latin – presumably arranged by his sisters in deference to his learning. Not something Petit himself would have done I would think. The full inscription is given in the biography. The others all have a few words but perhaps most poignant is his sister Louisa's, on the top. Louisa died aged 30 'released by merciful providence from a life of almost uninterrupted suffering… which she bore with true Christian patience and cheerfulness'.

8.11 Stowe Pool, ws13 6dw

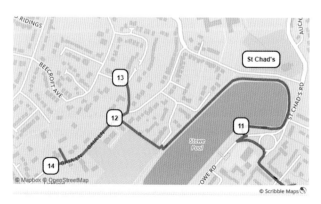

Either take the direct route down St Michael's Road past the side of Tesco (shorter), or return back to the Cathedral and, after passing the Minster pool, turn right before reaching the Close and you will come to another park, and Stowe pool.

This picture, 11, is interesting because it appears to show the pool drained of water and being dredged by a chain of workers. It cannot count among the better pictures

8.12. The Cathedral from Overstowe, 1857, 27 × 37. Not surprisingly, because of the similarity in treatment, this was completed just a month after Fig. 8.10.

elsewhere in this tour, being more of an unfinished sketch, uniformly reddish instead of finished with overlays of more colours. Dated 31 March 1857, it records the building, by an army of labourers, of the pool that we see today. The South Staffordshire Waterworks Company had taken over the area in 1856 and this was part of their undertaking. Previously there had been a millpond and the land around was quite boggy. One story of the origin of the name Lichfield is that 'lic' is a Saxon word for bog. Notice the view of the spires from this angle is no less impressive. To continue Petit's explanation:

> And on looking at the edifice from different points of view, the sense of fine proportion is not lost; it may be felt more in some points than others, but it never wholly leaves us. Even when from position the outline of one of the steeples is lost, the charm continues; we feel that we are looking at a finely proportioned structure...

If you have had enough of pictures of the Cathedral from every angle the short cut back to the car park is directly in front past the Cathedral. Otherwise just a few more, all lovely ones. Best is to walk around the far side of the pool where you see the church of St Chad. I have not yet found a Petit of

8.13b. The Cathedral from Gaia Fields, 1852 or 1853, 27 × 37. This album appears to have been completed in a very poor mood (see also the picture at Bilston 4.1). Petit returns to a previously favoured spot to paint the same view with eighteen years of decay.

8.13a. The Cathedral from Gaia Fields, c. 1835, 29 × 23. A favourite view back in the early days.

this church. In the nineteenth century it was still a small parish relative to St Mary's and St Michael's. Cedda, or St Chad, is said to have built his monk's cell there in 665, shortly after the kingdom of Mercia converted to Christianity and before the first Cathedral had been completed. There is a well said to be holy which was for a while a place of pilgrimage. Chad later became archbishop of Mercia, at a time when such positions did not carry all the trappings and elevated status of Norman times.

8.12–13 The Cathedral from Overstowe and Gaia Fields, WS13 7LR

The whole region above Stowe Pool was undeveloped in the mid-nineteenth century, with just one significant house and the Gaia fields, an ancient parcel of land that had belonged to the Cathedral since at least the thirteenth century.

Follow the path that goes uphill on the other side of Stowe Pool, keeping the sports field on your left. At the end you arrive in Gaia Lane. If you turn left in a few yards there is a raised entrance to a gate where you can see the exact angle, although a bit too close, for picture 12.

Head back the other way (if you have the energy, but you will need to return here, and there is no view to be seen) and turn up Bulldog Lane and there is an old house on the left called Overstowe. The next two pictures were made close by because the angle is very similar, and further away where I have not found a view. There is a stream here, which can be heard, and which may be the same one. Both are numbered 13, because they were drawn from the exact same spot, but twenty years apart, in about 1835 and in 1853. This was a favourite location for Petit because at least one other almost

8.14. The Cathedral from Bishop's Walk, 1868, 28 × 39. In his last years the pictures Petit did for relaxation are a riot of colour.

identical version from the 1830s is known – currently hanging in the Samuel Johnson Museum. The second picture, a rough sketch, is from 1852 or 1853, when the tree is clearly 20 years older. It was (perhaps obviously) drawn during a difficult period in Petit's life, when he was completing his third and most intense book *Architectural Studies in France*, and his mother and last brother had recently died, as we saw in the Cathedral. The two side-by-side show the effect of decay, reflected in events in his own family.

8.14 From Bishop's Walk

Return to Gaia Lane and walk a little further along towards the Cathedral, passing the junction with Bishop's Walk footpath, and you will come to a wall just low enough to peer over. You will see the old moat of the Cathedral, from exactly the correct angle, albeit a little closer. It was done in April of Petit's last year, 1868. And the view today of the moat from over the wall makes up for the lack of satisfaction in the previous picture.

The actual location where Petit sat, was, I think, a little further up Bishop's Walk where the angle is the same, although most of the view is obscured by the modern house.

As you peer over the wall notice the building just the other side of the moat and on the right. It looks remarkably like that in the picture, but that is unlikely, since it is below the level of Petit's one.

8.15. The Cathedral from Sandford Brook, 1867, 28 × 38. As colourful as the 1868 picture above.

It is noticeable how towards the end of his life the completed watercolours, albeit there are few of them, have a more aggressively colourful tone – lurid even. Artists with failing eyesight sometimes reacted in this way. We do not know in Petit's case.

8.15 FROM TRUNKFIELD BROOK, BLAKEMAN WAY WS13 8FL

Our last stop can be driven to easily enough on the way in or out of Lichfield, a very off-the-beaten-track part of the city. The view is mostly obscured by modern development and I include it mainly because it is the last of the series of completed, later, pictures of the Cathedral.

The Trunkfield Brook was formerly named Sandford Brook, possibly after a crossing nearby. The brook, and what remains of the ponds shown in the picture is across the small park at this postcode. But the view of the Cathedral and of St Mary's is better seen from the road, at least in summer. St Michael's is not visible at all now, as it was in the picture. There is, however, a footpath named Cathedral Walk that follows the line of the old brook all the way back to the Cathedral Close, which no doubt is how Petit came to this spot in August of 1867.

Quite likely it is Petit, or his sister, who sits in contemplation by the water's edge with a white cat nearby. They occasionally included each other in their sketches.

To conclude Petit's own description: 'The cathedral is not a large one, and perhaps the excellence of its proportions may make it appear smaller than it really is. I have rarely seen a satisfactory drawing of this cathedral, and I believe it to be a very difficult subject for the artist.' Both Turner and Girtin, and many less reputed artists, drew Lichfield cathedral in Petit's day, and many artists continue to try. The varied Petit pictures of Lichfield taken in one style from every angle, which were only uncovered in the last twenty years, provide a deeper appreciation of its unique architecture.

9.1.   Abbaye des Dames, Caen, Normandy, 1839, 24 × 30. The town of origin of Petit's ancestors, first visited by Petit in preparation for his first book, *Remarks*, in 1839.

The Reverend J. L. Petit: A Brief Biography

The Reverend John Louis Petit (1801–68) was a leading writer and speaker about church architecture, and a wonderfully original watercolour artist. Yet the opportunity for a reputation in either field was spoilt due to accidental, and deliberate, circumstances. For a period in the mid-nineteenth century he was the leading opponent of the Gothic craze for both restoration and the building of new churches. His position attracted vitriolic criticism and his views only prevailed after his death, and after most medieval churches had been modified. However, even his strongest critics valued the numerous impressionistic illustrations in watercolour that he brought back from his travels to all parts of the UK, Europe and the Middle East to complement his lectures and writing. Petit never sold his art in his lifetime, and it has become available just in the last 30 years. Only now can Petit's range of styles and his unique ability to capture the dignity and power of churches start to be appreciated.

FAMILY AND EARLY YEARS

The Petit family were moderately wealthy landowners, clergymen and intellectuals from Lichfield, Staffordshire. Four generations previously Louis Petit (1665–1720) of Caen, a cavalry captain, fled France following the Edict of Nantes and joined the army of Prince William of Orange, and thence to the British army where he rose to the rank of Brigadier General and Governor of Minorca. His son John Petit married the daughter of John Hayes, a wealthy solicitor from Tattenhall, who had accumulated a large estate of many parcels of land around Wolverhampton. Their son was a doctor and his son, John Louis Petit's father, was the first to take holy orders. The Reverend John Hayes Petit (1770–1822) was the permanent incumbent at Shareshill, while his brother, Petit's uncle, Louis Hayes Petit (1774–1849) was a London solicitor, member of the Society of Antiquaries and MP for Ripon.

John Louis Petit was the eldest of ten children, including two younger brothers who died before him, childless, and seven sisters, six of whom survived him, four who married, three with children: Harriet Salt, Mary Chetwynd and Maria Jelf. All the sisters painted. In particular Emma Gentile (1808–93) travelled and worked closely with her brother after 1845, even contributing occasional drawings to illustrate his writings, but most particularly cataloguing and organizing his work. However sisters Elizabeth, Mary Chetwynd, Maria Jelf, and his niece Sarah Salt, daughter of Harriet, also travelled with him on occasion and they too painted in a similar albeit weaker style. To make things somewhat confusing none of them signed their work.

9.2. The Brig, Harwich, c. 1834, 23 × 15. Petit's early shipping pictures were highly praised by Philip Delamotte.

9.3. The Regatta, Southend, c. 1832?, 16 x 33. Petit did attend this annual regatta in 1832, so the guess is not wholly without foundation.

9.4. Stadhuis, Ghent, 14 × 10cm, 1830–34. A similar picture from further back was drawn by Prout for a published series of lithographs from the Low Countries. Petit excludes the artfully placed people Prout uses in his compositions.

Petit married Louisa Reid (1806–88) in July 1828; they had no children. Louisa's health deteriorated very quickly and she was looked after for a long while by her unmarried sister, Amelia Reid, who also occasionally painted with Petit. Thus there are six women in Petit's circle whose sketches have been mistaken for his on occasion. Louisa was a good artist but she seems to have concentrated entirely on still life and in a very different style.

After graduating from Cambridge in 1825, Petit took holy orders in the same year and then worked, firstly as an assistant curate in St Michael's Lichfield for three years and then curate in the twin parishes of Bradfield and Mistley (near Harwich), Essex from 1828 until 1834. His wife Louisa's family was from Kent and Essex so it was no accident that he went there, and numerous early pictures are from those counties as well as Staffordshire. A newspaper cutting records Petit acting as steward for a nearby regatta in the 1830s and he painted quite a few shipping pictures in this period. He also travelled to Holland from the nearby port of Harwich and his earliest continental pictures date from this period.

9.5. Lisieux Cathedral, 1839, 28 × 21. This watercolour was copied for *Remarks*, vol 1, p. 138, but it is a much richer and more colourful picture than the architectural watercolours which Petit did in the UK just before, such as Hartington, Fig. 7.8

It is at this time, the early 1830s, that Petit's painting style takes a significant step forward under the influence of Samuel Prout – one of the most admired professional artists of the day, who had started to specialize in old continental buildings. Petit and Prout knew each other and perhaps Petit took lessons with Prout. Petit's buildings now start to have texture and he begins to master the dramatic angle that would be a distinguishing feature of his work. For several years in the mid-1830s his pictures are rather dark, almost black and white in some cases.

THE START OF PETIT'S ARTISTIC AND ARCHITECTURAL CAREER 1834–45

In 1834 Petit resigned his curacy and returned to the Midlands, first living near Shifnal in Shropshire. Presumably, being an intensely active man, it was with the intention of pursuing his twin vocations of drawing and writing about church architecture. Yet it would be seven years until his first book, *Remarks on Church Architecture* (*Remarks*), appeared in 1841. It appears

9.6. Eze, 1839, 21.5 × 25. One of the few landscapes drawn on this trip.

to have been conceived to counter the then exclusive preference for Neo-Gothic for restoring churches and building new ones. Modern Gothic had already established itself as a dominant fashion in church architecture since the late 1820s, and this would be further encouraged by Augustus Pugin's Gothic manifesto, *Contrasts*, (or to give it its full title, *Contrasts: Or, A Parallel Between the Noble Edifices of the Fourteenth and Fifteenth Centuries and Similar Buildings of the Present Day. Shewing the Present Decay of Taste. Accompanied by Appropriate Text*). This came out in 1835, and, as the full title implies, decreed 'the wonderful superiority of the Architectural Works of the Middle Ages' over those of the present day.

Petit's *Remarks* even now can be appreciated as an extraordinary achievement both architecturally and artistically, and it may well have occupied most of the seven years until its publication. The point, as he says in the introduction, is to demonstrate the profound beauty in all historical styles from across all Europe, and thus to demonstrate that it is unnecessarily restrictive for architects to limit themselves to copying one narrow period from this country.

Furthermore Petit was most concerned that medieval churches that existed should be altered only to the minimum extent necessary during repair and restoration for all the reasons that are obvious to us now 180 years later but which were certainly not accepted then. Whims of modern architects, or arbitrary rules, should not supersede the wisdom of generations, the harmony and dignity that centuries bring, and the associations for the community. Petit's art contributed the proof. The two volumes contain more than three hundred illustrations. He selected the best of the watercolours he had made on his tours and converted them into line drawings himself; those were then engraved for publication. Around one third were English examples (see Tixall, tour 1; Clifton, tour 3; Tong, tour 4; Leigh, tour 5; Norbury, tour 6 and Hartington, tour 7 for examples shown in *Remarks*), a third from France, and the other third from the Low Countries, along the Rhine, Switzerland, Italy and

9.7. Payerne, Switzerland, 1837–39, 13 × 18. A continental landscape showing light effects similar to those developed around Ashbourne in 1838.

elsewhere in Britain. Gradually the austere look of the early to mid-thirties gave way to some of the most colourful art of his entire life in the final trip to France in 1839 – presumably as the book came to fulfilment, three such continental watercolours from this time are shown here.

Highly praised by those who were not convinced by the Gothicists, and concerned about conservation, it faced vitriolic criticism from members of the recently started Ecclesiological Society who wanted to lay down restrictive rules based on Pugin. This battle, 'the battle of the styles', continued for the rest of Petit's life. An early concrete example of the argument from the 1840s concerned the proposed restoration of St Mary's, the principal church of Stafford, by a youngish George Gilbert Scott. Petit opposed as unnecessary the return to sloping roofs on the south transept (see tour 2 for more discussion and pictures around this).

Criticism from the Ecclesiologists included that beauty had no place in matters of religion; and any use of foreign 'pagan' models would be abhorrent on principle. Probably as a consequence Petit's second book in 1845 (actually a publication of a speech) makes the same points as in *Remarks* but focusing just on historical English styles, and with the art a little toned down to focus on the importance of preserving architectural character rather than beauty (see Rugeley, tour 1 and Pattingham, tour 3 for pictures from this book).

9.8. Langrune, 1851, 26 × 34. An architectural sketch reproduced
in Petit's second book: *Architectural Studies in France*, 1854, p. 154.
Much more serious in tone than those for the first book.

LEADERSHIP OF THE 'ANTI-GOTHIC PARTY' 1845–60S

Antiquarians and ecclesiologists opposed to 'one correct style' formed the Archaeological Society
in 1844, and started the *Archaeological Journal*, where Petit was one of the most frequent contribu-
tors. Seventeen of his articles were published there alone. From this time he also delivered frequent
speeches up and down the country, five of which were published as small books, and some others
are recorded in the *Transactions* of annual meetings of the Archaeological Society. By the late 1840s
Petit was simultaneously receiving praise as the only architectural critic worth reading (Professor
Freeman), and being branded as an enthusiastic amateur by gothic architects and those wishing to
discredit him (in the important weekly *The Builder*). Though even his fiercest critics acknowledged
the great merit in his sketches and illustrations, for conveying both remarkable accuracy, and 'effect',

9.9. Saint-Front, Perigueux, France, 1852, 23 × 28. Also reproduced in *Architectural Studies in France*, p. 67.

a word used frequently in those days to convey the overall impression of the building, including the emotional and spiritual impression.

Gradually the arguments evolved. As architects and other writers travelled so the scorn for foreign models and stricture of one true type of Gothic (but still Gothic) lessened. But for Petit this was not enough and he embarked on a major task to find specific examples of beautiful round arch styles in regions of France at the boundary between the Gothic north and Roman south: *Architectural Studies in France*. Aimed at the more limited audience of church architects and commentators, the field work was carried out mainly in 1851 and 1852, the legacy of which was some three hundred sketches of otherwise often obscure churches from Paris to Bordeaux. This seemed to have cemented his reputation, in that disparagement, in *The Builder* for example, turned to admiration. Henceforth he was seen as one of the leaders of the anti-Gothic faction. He was still strongly

9.10. Hambye Abbey, Normandy, 1863, 27 × 38. A closer view of the abbey was reproduced in the Ilam Anastatic Drawing Society album of 1867. Petit's later wider views can be fully finished as opposed to sketches which focus on architecture close up, which were often left with just reddish washes.

opposed and occasionally deliberately mis-construed by Scott, Street and the other Gothicists, an indication of his importance in the debate.

Philip Delamotte, one of the pioneers of photography in Britain, was by this time a close collaborator and friend. Originally helping with preparing illustrations for articles in the *Archaeological Journal*, he contributed forty-five of the 130 illustrations in *Architectural Studies*, and on occasion he travelled with Petit. Later, as Professor of Art at Kings College, Delamotte would write *The Art of Sketching from Nature*, referring often to Petit alongside the great professional watercolourists.

Petit was elected a Fellow of the Society of Antiquaries, admitted *ad eundem* to the University of Oxford, was an honorary member of the Archaeological Institute, and of the Institute of British Architects (later the RIBA), as well as holding regional positions such as Secretary of the Lichfield Architectural Society and President of the Lichfield Working Men's Association.

The RIBA sponsored annual Architectural Exhibitions for a wider audience in the 1850s and 1860s where Petit was one of the most frequent lecturers and exhibitors, for example his speech on

9.11. Pantocrator, Constantinople, undated, 23 × 32. A drawing made to exhibit at a lecture, possibly at the RIBA in 1858, and also reproduced in the *Archaeological Journal* article 1865.

'Utilitarianism in Architecture' in 1855, quoted in tour 4, and drawings of his own house shown in tour 1.

At the same time he continued to deliver papers pursuing his themes of inspiring originality through breadth of example – for example on Italian [church] architecture in 1855 and on Byzantine [religious] architecture in 1858, following a short trip to Greece and Constantinople in 1857. He continued to travel further and further afield, covering Spain and the Mediterranean islands in 1858; and he made a lengthy tour to Egypt and Syria in 1864/5.

Petit was aged sixty at the time of his speech, 'On the Revival of Styles', given at the Architectural Exhibition in 1861. Despite having seen the debate move substantially towards conservatism in restoration, and in favour of originality rather than copy Gothic, he was still battling against the exclusive preference for work based on Gothic, now not just for ecclesiastical structures but for secular too.

'Without for a moment depreciating the grandeur of a fine Gothic interior, I must observe that the Classic style contains elements of at least equal grandeur, if not greater,' and backing this up with

9.12. Dinon, 1854, 26 × 36cm. A finished watercolour of the later period, compare with those of Lichfield in Tour 8, for example.

remarkably technical comparisons of different features and an extraordinary range of examples, which would have been illustrated with his own watercolours around the walls of the lecture hall.

In every year from 1851, when reasonable records start, he travelled both in the UK and abroad, completing between one hundred (1866) and five hundred (1854) sketches, but mostly around two hundred and fifty. Some of these are unfinished, never going beyond the first reddish wash, and many are architectural notes, capturing just the essential details of a building, but many in each year were finished for exhibition at his speeches or, relatively rarely, for his own pleasure. Among the latter one supposes are the sketches of Lichfield cathedral (see tour 8). While there is a reason he painted it thirty times in 1857 alone – it was just before the restoration by Gilbert Scott began – in most years he painted it several times, presumably for the pleasure and relaxation of doing it again, from a different angle or to try out variations of style and effect.

Petit was neither professional academic, nor architect, in an age when it was still possible for such work to be led by amateurs. He undertook designs for some alterations in St Paul's, being one of its few defenders in the Neo-Gothic age; and in 1861/2 designed and supervised the construction of

9.13. Caerdeon Chapel, 1866, 27 × 38. Four years after its completion. One may detect a little justifiable pride in this picture.

one small church – St Philip's Caerdeon, for his brother-in-law, the Reverend William Jelf. True to himself, it is one of the few original designs of a church from that time, and is indeed one of a kind, although predictably the Ecclesiologist was scathing. Despite a tiny congregation, it still stands, with grade I protection, on a wooded hillside overlooking the estuary near Barmouth in North Wales.

Petit died, apparently from a chill caught while sketching, in December 1868. The epitaph on the side of the family vault reads:

CUJUS INGENIUM NULLI SECUNDUM PŒNE OMNIA COMPLECTENS
MODESTIÆ BENEVOLENTIÆ LIBERALITATI LONGE CESSIT
CUJUS HUMILEM IN DEO FIDEM
FERVIDUS ERGA HOMINES AMOR
CONTINUE ET FIDELITER EXPRESSIT
ILLUM OMNES AMANTEM AB OMNIBUS AMATUM
AD CHRISTI DECEDENTEM GREMIUM
DIE 2 DEC 1868 ÆTS SUAE 67
PIO OMNES PROSEQUIMUR DESIDERIO PROSEQUEMUR

To summarise, it says that he was as modest, generous and kind as he was brilliant; humble and faithful; loving and loved by all. It is the first part that seems exceptional and well chosen from all that I have read about him.

POSTHUMOUS DISPARAGEMENT

9.14. Cartmel Priory, 1868, 27 × 37. A sketch, yet more than a sketch, which captures the effect of the Priory in the village. This was reproduced in Petit's posthumous article in the *Archaeological Journal* about the Priory.

After his death the 1869 Architectural Exhibition gave over its main exhibition room to an exhibition of 339 of his watercolours. The *Archaeological Journal* published a further three of his articles posthumously, and his sister published his lengthy poem, 'The Greater and The Lesser Light', which attempts to reconcile religious belief with understanding derived from the rapid scientific developments of the age.

Yet, despite these few positive developments, and Delamotte including him alongside Turner, Cotman, and the other great artists of earlier in the century in his book, overall Petit's reputation, both as an architectural commentator and as an artist, has suffered hugely since his death. In the battle of styles his opponents were all younger and able to continue writing and rewriting history to suit their own legacies. To give just one example Gilbert Scott, in his memoirs remembered Petit 'with affection', for 'his noble character' and 'wonderful sketches', but seemingly Scott employed this praise as cover for finally dismissing Petit's architectural commentary in a way that he had repeatedly failed to do in his lifetime. William Morris *et al* started the Society for the Protection of Ancient Buildings in the 1870s but saw little reason to acknowledge Petit's, or others', tireless campaigning for the same ends.

Later Nikolaus Pevsner, the foremost architectural historian of the mid-twentieth century, although intellectually rigorous to the extreme himself, preferred to focus on the emotional drama and very specific style recommendations of Ruskin's writings, the Ecclesiologists, Pugin and Scott to Petit's rational eclecticism, and appears to have read only a little of his first book. For a while other historians would follow Pevsner's lead.

9.15. Fribourg, by Emma Petit, 26 September 1856, 24 × 30. A comparison with her brother's painting of the same subject on the same day, it is not one of Emma's best perhaps, but the few better ones seem to have Petit's help.

9.16. Fribourg, 26 September 1856, 26 × 36. The real thing. Notice especially how solid and substantial is the cathedral, by comparison with Emma's version.

As an artist the story has been, if anything, even worse. The chairmanship of the Architectural Exhibition Society was taken over by a Petit opponent before the exhibition of Petit's pictures, which was thoroughly mishandled, with no explanations or organization to the display. After this there is no evidence that Emma tried to do anything else with the huge collection that Petit left. Eight hundred works went to other family members, the vast majority, estimated at 10–15,000 including drawings for illustration, all the early albums of his most finished watercolours, and sketches, stayed together. Petit's pictures were stored, after Emma, by a nephew William Jelf-Petit and subsequently his only daughter, Elsie, for a hundred years. The hoard was raided for trinkets occasionally and many deteriorated with damp (see example from Bilston, the first in tour 4 and Lichfield, tour 8, picture 8). They were left abandoned after the great-niece's death in 1957 in an old house in Surrey. The new owners, no doubt surprised by their luck, did nothing for a few years then gradually dumped the remains of the hoard into auctions, mostly through Sotheby's Billingshurst. The last 1500 or so in 1999. The auctioneers could think of nothing better than to sell them off in lots of a hundred or more for a few hundred pounds per lot, Petit's mixed up with those of his sisters.

We can compare an example of Emma's work, alongside that of her brother. There are no such examples from Staffordshire because she travelled with him mostly on his foreign forays from the 1850s. Both of these were done on the same day, 26 September 1856. Judging by the angles, they were sitting fairly close together on the same road. The one above is overly colourful, but more importantly the architecture is inaccurate and lacks substance. It has Emma's handwriting on the back but it, and hundreds of others like it, were sold as Petit. The one below has Petit's writing and catalogue number on the back and is altogether different in quality and character.

9.17. Puss and Puff, Bymblekyte, 1867, 27 × 37.

Petit was undoubtedly a very important figure in the story of church architecture in the nineteenth century, but recognition of his role relies on a relatively small group of architectural historians. Appreciating his art, on the other hand, is for a much wider potential audience. However, that is not straightforward in a period when representative art is not fashionable, and when he has already been forgotten, and because of the confusion surrounding his family circle. One must look past the clutter of Emma and the rest's weaker efforts and set aside the unfinished architectural notes. What is left is a most extraordinary artistic record of the mid-nineteenth century, even if only half the work has survived to our times.

Like another multi-talented mid-Victorian, Edward Lear, his early work is clearly grounded in the art of the time, while his later work goes off on a track of its own. In Petit's case this is much closer to the Impressionism of France, where he most frequently travelled, than the elaborate detail, colour and composition of the Pre-Raphaelites, praised by Ruskin, which took British art in an altogether different direction.

Unlike the work of commercial artists his watercolours are not contrived, carefully composed or artificially picturesque in any of the ways that can make Victorian pictures seem old-fashioned. His pictures record what was there, not what patrons wanted to see. They aim to convey effect and character; factual but not just a statement of fact as in earlier antiquarian topography. Always impressionistic, sometimes unfinished or rough, perhaps they can be appreciated in our time more easily than the finished compositions of his contemporaries. Petit's unique gift was to communicate the majesty, power and solemnity of ancient churches of all sizes and styles, and their relation to the communities in which they stand, and to treat landscapes in a similar way – as the works of God. His pictures demonstrate exactly his belief in the vital importance of harmony and beauty in our religious buildings and in nature. His conviction was that no one style or landscape need be raised above all others, and that they all must be protected. That is what drove him to paint.

9.17. Loches, Indre-et-Loire, France, April 1854, 27 × 38. An impressionistic style that is wholly Petit's own.

Sources and Acknowledgements

Many individuals have helped and I have drawn on many sources. Rather than burden a travel guide with footnotes, the most important are listed here by tour, and at the end. All remaining mistakes are my own of course.

INTRODUCTION AND GENERAL

The inspiration and most important sources are Petit's own writings. He almost certainly would have kept personal papers, and his sisters would have preserved them until their deaths in the 1890s, but I have not yet located any such papers and they may have been destroyed. His published books, articles and a few letters in other archives are available. The most important of these are the three main books: *Remarks on Church Architecture* (1841); *Remarks on Architectural Character* (1846); *Architectural Studies in France* (1854); and the articles in the *Archaeological Journal* and *Transactions of the RIBA Council*.

The literature around the Gothic Revival is vast, I do not pretend to have read it all. The top three which I drew on are as follows: for the role played by the Ecclesiologists, the collection of essays by various authors in Christopher Webster and John Elliott, *'A Church as it Should Be.' The Cambridge Camden Society and its Influence* (Stamford: Shaun Tyas, 2000); for an overview of the Gothic Revival, Kenneth Clark's early work is hard to beat: Kenneth Clark, *The Gothic Revival* (Harmondsworth: Pelican, 1964); and for the other leading characters' works, Nikolaus Pevsner's *Some Architectural Writers of the Nineteenth-century* (Oxford: Oxford University Press, 1972), even though his appreciation of Petit was inadequate. For those wanting a quicker and easier introduction Wikipedia's page on Victorian Restoration is very readable.

For Staffordshire history I have used the Gazetteer mentioned in the text throughout: William White, *History, Directory and Gazetteer of Staffordshire*, 1834 (available online), and multiple internet sources and local history websites. The information on p. 10 about the numbers of churches built and restored is from Chapter 1 of Chris Brooks and Andrew Saint, *The Victorian Church* (Manchester: Manchester University Press, 1995). The characterization of Victorian gentlemen's education and activity on p. 13 is from Phillippa Levine, *The Amateur and The Professional* (Cambridge: Cambridge University Press, 1986). Wikipedia shortened the time required for research hugely and would otherwise be mentioned at almost every stop.

There are of course numerous guides to churches and other places noted in these tours. Usually I have taken information from the locations' own websites or those of local historical associations.

TOUR 1

Among the historical websites I would especially note that of the Staffordshire and Worcestershire canal, and the Ridware History Association.

The research on what became of Petit's house, Bumblekyte, in Upper Longdon was carried out entirely by Gareth Evans, whose family live in the Grange, and was published in a local parish publication.

Augustus Hare's Diary is called simply *The Story of My Life* and is available online. Originally it was published in 1896 in multiple volumes. His visit to the Petits and Salts occurs early in volume II.

Marion Kettle contributed the picture of Beaudesert Hall and helped in understanding Cannock Chase.

TOUR 2

The dispute around the restoration of St Mary's, Stafford, is well recorded, and unfortunately about the only incident in Petit's career which is widely noted. Gilbert Scott's version, in which he admits that it led to a much more conservative approach thereafter, and that he might have done things differently later, was included in a book on the restoration by J. Masfen of 1852 and is to be found in the Society of Antiquaries Library, pointed up to me by Chris Miele. Chris' essay on Victorian church restoration and the Ecclesiologists, pp.257–94 in the Webster and Elliott collection cited above, provides a much more detailed and nuanced description of their influence and attitudes to restoration, and the importance of St Mary's. I have simplified both throughout.

TOUR 3

The historical website for Burton on Trent is an amazing resource for the developments concerning the Bridge and the history of the town, as is the Robinson Garden website on the history of dovecotes.

Petit's comments on Clifton Campville are from volume II of *Remarks*.

A number of unnamed individuals were helpful, at the Whittington Golf Clubhouse allowing me to wander around the course; and especially in Netherseal looking at the Dovecote and for the distant church spire.

TOUR 4

The Black Country and St Peter's websites were important resources but less so than the individuals who drew on their own knowledge. My thanks to Sophie Heath, Collections Officer of the Museum at Wolverhampton City Council and Brendan Flynn, former curator, and Barry Sharman, local historian; who have contributed an appreciation of the rarity of Petit's watercolours of the area. The City of Wolverhampton also contributed an image of their watercolour. I am grateful to Christine Buckley for information concerning Petit's ownership of land around Ettingshall and the Sedgeley Beacon.

Petit's own appreciation of industrial architecture is from a public speech 'On Utilitarianism in Architecture' in 1856 at the Architectural Exhibition, reprinted in *The Builder*.

Petit's article on Tong was published in the *Archaeological Journal* in March 1845, and the one on Gloucester churches in 1847

The Reverend Rachel Livesey and the church warden kindly arranged access for me to the tower of Lapley church.

Tour 5

Petit's discussion of windows, and the illustration given is around page 175 in volume 1 of *Remarks*. His comments on Gothic which I quote at Croxden, come in the concluding chapter of his third book *Architectural Studies in France*.

The Alton Towers website includes a useful history page.

Tour 6

Whereas Petit's early pictures can be hard to date, at least two albums from 1838 had the year, and in some cases the month, written in Petit's own hand on each page.

Petit's comments on Norbury church can be found on page 102, volume II, of *Remarks*.

Mrs Liz Bownes of the The Dove Valley Arts Society and Mr Tony Spybey kindly read this and the following tour in the north of the county and made several helpful suggestions.

Tour 7

Petit's efficient logistics for watercolouring on the spot, and the great importance of such details as the type of bag, and easel, come from Philip Delamotte, *The Art of Sketching from Nature* (George Bell and sons, 1888). Delamotte was a pioneer of photography in the UK, Professor of Art at Kings College, London, was a close friend of Petit, and contributed sketches for Petit's third book.

The existence of Petit's slim volume of poetry comes as rather a shock after getting acquainted with his art and architectural commentary. It was noticed by the *Gentleman's Magazine* as another example, if one were needed, of Petit's extraordinary range of talents, but I expect it was a shock for contemporaries too.

The other poem is from volume II of *Remarks*. It is an isolated occurrence towards the end of the book and did not seem to arouse much comment.

Tour 8

Petit's description of the remarkable character and proportions of Lichfield Cathedral, quoted in several places, come from a lecture to the Northampton Mechanical Institute in 1853.

The quotes from Augustus Hare's diary are from *The Story of My Life,* Volume II, a few pages after the quotes in Tour 1.

The letters in *The Builder* referred to are from issues in February and March 1856.

The Samuel Johnson Birthplace Museum's (SJBM) album of Petit's sister is an invaluable resource for separating Petit's work from his circle's whose work is often misattributed to him. I am grateful to Joanne Wilson the curator of the SJBM for this, and for reading and commenting on this tour.

Local websites were more than averagely helpful for example in confirming the date of the dredging of Stowe pool.

Trevor James, Lay Reader at St Michael's and editor of *The Historian* helped in pointing to the resources to locate Petit's grave, as did Tony Briggs, the Town Clerk. Trevor also helped personally to make the vault more presentable to visitors who might stop for a glance at it, and in showing me the plaque to Petit's uncle inside the church. Lesley Allen and the Venerable George Frost, retired archdeacon, pointed me to the brass inside the cathedral to Petit's brother.

BIOGRAPHY

In addition to the sources referred to above, Petit's first obituary appeared in January 1869 in the *The Builder*, written by Albert Hartshorne, son of Petit's friend, the Reverend Charles Hartshorne, later editor of the *Archaeological Journal*. Subsequent published biographies all contain errors, including the brief notes in Cambridge University alumni database and the 2005 issue of the Oxford Dictionary of National Biography. For example by suggesting he worked as a priest in Bradfield in the later 1830s or 1840s when the dates were 1828–34.

Good sources of biographical and other information were the Church of England's Database of Clergy; Geneological Records; the British Newspaper Archive; Staffordshire Records Office; Northamptonshire Archives; the John Rylands Library archives in Manchester. Professor Alexandrina Buchanan pointed me to these archives. Her biography, *Robert Willis and the Foundation of Architectural History* (Woodbridge: Boydell Press, 2013), provided much context. The description of Pugin's *Contrasts* as a manifesto, and the short quote, is from Rosemary Hill's biography, *God's Architect* (London: Allen Lane, 2007). George Gilbert Scott's comments about Petit are from Gavin Stamp's edited version of Scott's *Personal and Professional Recollections* (Stamford: Paul Watkins, 1995) p. 298. I have published two recent articles in scholarly journals: 'The Rev'd Petit and the Beauty of Churches', *British Art Journal*, Vol. xviii, No. 2, November 2017, and 'The Rev'd Petit Standing up to the Neo-Gothicists', *Ecclesiology Today*, No. 55–56, May 2018.

The publisher, RPS Publications, is part of the Reverend Petit Society, a non-profit society set up to widen appreciation of Petit and his achievements. For more information about Petit or RPS see www.revpetit.com

Five individuals need special acknowledgement for their help in bringing this book to fruition: Sally Salvesen, editor, whose knowledge and experience of art publishing has been invaluable; Robin Simon, editor of the *British Art Journal*, who was among the first to recognise Petit's worth; Chris Copp, Senior Museums Officer at Staffordshire County Council, read and offered suggestions to half the tours, especially informing me about windmill sail rigging (for tour 2), as well as arranging the images of Staffordshire's Petit watercolours, 11 of which are used here. Ian Cooke, one of the biggest collectors of Petit, allowed me freely to choose whichever I wanted to use, and his fourteen pictures greatly improve tours 2 and 4. Lastly my wife Anna, who shares my enthusiasm for the artist and for bringing him to a wider audience.

Index

Bold = location visited in a tour
* = illustration